**New Directions for
Student Services**

Susan R. Jones
Co-Editor

Sherry K. Watt
Co-Editor

D1291926

Engaging the Digital Generation

Edmund T. Cabellon
Josie Ahlquist
Editors

Number 155 • Autumn 2016
Jossey-Bass
San Francisco

ENGAGING THE DIGITAL GENERATION
Edmund T. Cabellon, Josie Ahlquist (eds.)
New Directions for Student Services, no. 155

Susan R. Jones, Co-Editor
Sherry K. Watt, Co-Editor

NEW DIRECTIONS FOR STUDENT SERVICES (ISSN 0164-7970, e-ISSN 1536-0695) is part of The Jossey-Bass Higher and Adult Education Series and is published quarterly by Wiley Subscription Services, Inc., A Wiley Company, at Jossey-Bass, One Montgomery Street, Suite 1200, San Francisco, CA 94104-4594. POSTMASTER: Send address changes to New Directions for Student Services, Jossey-Bass, One Montgomery Street, Suite 1200, San Francisco, CA 94104-4594.

New Directions for Student Services is indexed in CIJE: Current Index to Journals in Education (ERIC), Contents Pages in Education (T&F), Current Abstracts (EBSCO), Education Index /Abstracts (H.W. Wilson), Educational Research Abstracts Online (T&F), ERIC Database (Education Resources Information Center), and Higher Education Abstracts (Claremont Graduate University).

Microfilm copies of issues and articles are available in 16 mm and 35 mm, as well as microfiche in 105 mm, through University Microfilms Inc., 300 North Zeeb Road, Ann Arbor, Michigan 48106-1346.

SUBSCRIPTIONS cost $89 for individuals in the U.S., Canada, and Mexico, and $113 in the rest of the world for print only; $89 in all regions for electronic only; and $98 in the U.S., Canada, and Mexico for combined print and electronic; and $122 for combined print and electronic in the rest of the world. Institutional print only subscriptions are $335 in the U.S., $375 in Canada and Mexico, and $409 in the rest of the world; electronic only subscriptions are $335 in all regions; and combined print and electronic subscriptions are $402 in the U.S., $442 in Canada and Mexico, and $476 in the rest of the world.

EDITORIAL CORRESPONDENCE should be sent to the Co-Editors, Susan R. Jones, The Ohio State University, 310D Ramseyer Hall, 29 W. Woodruff Ave., Columbus, OH 43210; and Sherry K. Watt, The University of Iowa, N485 Lindquist Center, Iowa City, IA 52242.

Cover design: Wiley
Cover Images: © Lava 4 images | Shutterstock

www.josseybass.com

CONTENTS

Editors' Notes

Higher education has drastically changed throughout this millennium, represented in part, by the shift in student demographics and variety of institutions offering traditional and innovative credentials. Of these changes, *digital* technology's impact continues to be researched and its applications implemented throughout administrative practice. When we were first approached to produce this volume of *New Directions for Student Services*, we wanted to expand the focus beyond students and include practitioners. Engaging the *digital generation* is not a certain population or demographic, but addresses a collective shift. Users are seeking out, utilizing, remixing technology tools for a variety of reasons, all impacting our global society. The field of student affairs, both professionals and those students we serve, are included in this digital generation.

In 2015, two-thirds of American adults owned a smartphone of some kind, an increase from just one-third of adults in 2011 (Smith, 2015). In addition, smartphones augmented personal computers and laptops, increasing content creation and moderation among college students, ages 18–29 (Cabellon & Junco, 2015). In fact, these students produced more Internet content, to include social networking posts, music, and videos, than any other age demographic (Junco, 2014). Perrin and Duggan (2015) posited that data from 2000 to 2015 highlighted several key trends; most notably, that young adults (ages 18–29) with high levels of education, have reached Internet saturation. Looking at social media applications, in 2015 the most popular platform was Facebook, with research finding 90–99% college students logging on daily (Chen & Marcus, 2012; Pempek, Yermolayeva, & Calvert, 2009). This high usage was also a major finding in the 2015 Pew Research Center Americans' Internet Access report, which documents that 96% of youth from 18–29 use the Internet. This edition considers youths' use of social tools, but the number of adults and educational professionals online is also rising. This same Pew study found that 84% of adults used the Internet in 2015, compared to only 52% in 2000 (Smith, 2015).

The challenge of producing a text about technology use in student affairs is keeping up with technology's rapid change and acknowledging varying perceptions. By the time this edition is released, modifications to applications and their impact will have evolved. Technologies are quickly transforming our society and our institutions at a pace that educators may not be comfortable. At the same time, stories about social media being used to threaten or deceive others flood the news. To obtain the most updated information, scholarship and content on technology, a variety of sources were included from academic journals, books, recently defended dissertations, as well as technology related blog posts. A through line in this edition is

New Directions for Student Services, no. 155, Autumn 2016 © 2016 Wiley Periodicals, Inc.
Published online in Wiley Online Library (wileyonlinelibrary.com) • DOI: 10.1002/ss.20179

the integration of the newly approved ACPA and NASPA technology (Tech) competency. The Tech competency is defined as follows:

> Focuses on the use of digital tools, resources, and technologies for the advancement of student learning, development, and success as well as the improved performance of student affairs professionals. Included within this area are knowledge, skills, and dispositions that lead to the generation of digital literacy and digital citizenship within communities of students, student affairs professionals, faculty members, and colleges and universities as a whole. (ACPA & NASPA, 2015, p. 15) This competency gives further weight to this volume, declaring that student affairs technology is no longer an option but integrated into the work student affairs administrators do. The purpose of this edition is not only to focus on the current tools or technology trends, but also the practices, possibilities and direction to integrate and embrace a technology-open mindset into the work of a student affairs educator.

As we took on the responsibility for editing this *New Directions for Student Services (NDSS)* volume, we reached out to some of the most innovative scholar practitioners to highlight important trends and research that influenced changes in administrative practice. In fact, as the volume took shape, we decided to start the volume with a focus on administrators and educators before focusing on the students we serve. We were intentional with a focus on senior student affairs officers, knowing that these administrators would be the catalysts to move the academy forward.

Our goal with this volume is to elevate student affairs administrators' sophistication using digital technologies. The topics are interconnected and challenge the reader to move beyond what they already know and inspire professionals to do more. The complexities of digital technology implementation and its impact on students, faculty, and staff are evident; yet, we have an obligation to not only discover new ways to utilize digital technology with our students, but with our colleagues across the academy as well.

To this end, in Chapter 1, Ed Cabellon and Julie Payne-Kirchmeier present a historical perspective on how student affairs professionals used digital technology over the past ten years and how this history could impact the next generation of student affairs professionals. Then, Josie Ahlquist proposes an important, holistic framework for digital identity development as student affairs professionals in Chapter 2. In Chapter 3, Kara Kolomitz and Ed Cabellon describe the strategic importance of senior student affairs officers (SSAOs) leading with a digital mindset through increased digital fluency.

After Chapter 3, the volume shifts focus to understanding the student experience and student engagement in the digital age. In Chapter 4, Paul Gordon Brown explores how digital and social technologies may be impacting the developmental journeys of traditionally aged college students and explores the application of college student development theory in digital spaces. Liz Gross and Jason Meriwether discuss strategies and tools for student services professionals to leverage digital data to measure student engagement and learning outcomes in Chapter 5. The volume then concludes with Chapter 6, which describes how to effectively establish social media guidelines and policies for colleges and universities. Laura Pasquini outlines effective practical approaches for its creation and implementation for the entire campus community, including students, faculty, and administrators.

Finally, readers will discover as part of our Editor's Notes, a "Definition of Terms" section. We hope that this helps contextualize vernacular common to our author team, but may not be as common to those professionals still growing in their understanding of digital technology topics in higher education settings.

After reading this volume, we call upon our colleagues across the academy to acknowledge their current technological biases and discuss with their colleagues on and off campus how student affairs practice might be redefined using digital technology more intentionally. We are grateful to our colleagues who contributed to this volume and hope those who read it discover new ways digital and social technologies enhance their student affairs work.

Defining Digital Technology Terminology

Digital Technology: An associated electronic infrastructure of access and transport: a public framework for transmission, exchange, and participation. Arguably, the technology of the digital, in this sense of its mechanism for access, is one starting point for a deeper consideration of digital artifacts as cultural phenomena (Crook, 2013, p. 27).

Digital Identity. The term digital identity is not to be confused with a developmental construct within identity development theory. Rather, it is the online presentation of self, including how one chooses to use social media tools. This behavior is known in the research as self-presentation, defined as "the conscious or unconscious process by which people try to influence the perception of their image, typically through social interactions" (Junco, 2014, p. 111). Digital identities may possess digital reputations, or reputations that arise from how others view these digital identities (Brown, 2016).

Digital Leadership. In the field of K–12 education, one source proposes that, "Digital leadership focuses on a consistent pursuit of innovation, effective integration of technology, quality of professional development, transparency, celebration of success from which others may learn, establishment of relationships with stakeholders, an open mind, and anticipation of continued change" (Sheninger, 2014, p. 23). In higher education, Ahlquist (2016) created a digital leadership framework based upon a holistic digital identity, including prioritizing relationships, strategic communications, leadership philosophy, and embracing change.

Social Media. "Social Media is the arena where users can engage in the creation and development of content and gather online to share knowledge, information, opinions using web-based applications, and tools" (Grover & Stewart, 2010, p. 9). Kaplan and Haelien (2010) also acknowledged the power that users have, defining social media specifically as "a group of internet-based applications that build on the ideological and technological foundations of Web 2.0 and that allow the creation and exchange of User Generated Content (UGC)" (p. 61).

Social Networking Sites (SNS). The term "social networking sites" is an umbrella term used to describe online, electronic communication tools, such as Facebook, Twitter, and Instagram that allowed individuals to construct profiles, display user connections, share information, and search within a list of said connections (boyd & Ellison, 2007).

Web 2.0. An "active and open web architecture that enables users to participate in facilitating active learning" (Birnbaum, 2013 p. 2). At first, these tools included methods from computer-mediated communication that were not previously available, including e-mail, chat rooms, list serves, text messaging, and some social media tools.

Edmund T. Cabellon
Josie Ahlquist
Editors

References

Ahlquist, J. (2016). *Digitally connected: Exploring the social media utilization of senior-level student affairs administrators.* Manuscript submitted for publication.

boyd, d. m., & Ellison, N. B. (2007). Social networking sites: Definition, history, and scholarship. *Journal of Computer-Mediated Communication, 13*(1), 210–230.

Brown, P. G. (2016). *College students, social media, digital identities, and the digitized self (Doctoral dissertation).* Boston College, Chestnut Hill, MA.

Birnbaum, M. (2013). The fronts students use: Facebook and the standardization of self presentations. *Journal of College Student Development, 54*(2), 155–171.

Cabellon, E. T., & Junco, R. (2015). The digital age of student affairs. In E. Whitt & J. Schuh (Eds.), *New directions for student services, 1997–2014: Glancing back, looking forward* (pp. 49–61). San Francisco, CA: Jossey-Bass.

Chen, B., & Marcus, J. (2012). Students' self-presentation on Facebook: An examination of personality and self-construal factors. *Computers in Human Behavior, 28*(6), 2091–2099.

College Student Educators International (ACPA) & Student Affairs Professionals in Higher Education (NASPA). (2015). *Professional competency areas for student affairs educators.* Retrieved from http://www.naspa.org/images/uploads/main/ACPA_NASPA_Professional_Competencies_FINAL.pdf

Crook, C. (2013). The field of digital technology research. In S. Price, C. Jewitt, & B. Brown (Eds.), *The SAGE handbook of digital technology research* (pp. 26–40). Thousand Oaks, CA: Sage.

Grover, A., & Stewart, D. W. (2010). Defining interactive social media in an educational context. In C. Wankel (Ed.), *Cutting edge social media approaches to business education: Teaching with LinkedIN, Facebook. Twitter, Second Life, and Blogs* (pp. 7–38). Charlotte, NC: Information Age Publishing.

Kaplan, A. M., & Haenlein, M. (2010). Users of the world, unite! The challenges and opportunities of social media. *Business Horizons, 53*(1), 59–68.

Junco, R. (2014). *Engaging students through social media: Evidence-based practices for use in student affairs.* San Francisco, CA: Jossey-Bass.

Pempek, T. A., Yermolayeva, Y. A., & Calvert, S. L. (2009). College students' social networking experiences on Facebook. *Journal of Applied Developmental Psychology, 30,* 227–238.

Sheninger, E. (2014). *Digital Leadership: Changing paradigms for changing times.* Thousand Oaks, CA: Corwin A Sage Company.

Smith, A. (2015, April 1). U.S. device use in 2015. *Pew Research Center.* Retrieved from http://www.pewinternet.org/2015/04/01/us-device-use-in-2015/

EDMUND T. CABELLON *is the assistant to the vice president of student affairs and enrollment management at Bridgewater State University and the former co-chair of ACPA's Presidential Task Force on Digital Technology.*

JOSIE AHLQUIST *is an adjunct faculty at Florida State University, Undergraduate Certificate in Leadership Studies program and independent digital leadership educator and researcher.*

NEW DIRECTIONS FOR STUDENT SERVICES • DOI: 10.1002/ss

1

This chapter provides a historical perspective of student affairs professionals' use of digital and social technologies in their work on college campuses. The purpose of the chapter is to describe how digital technology tools have evolved since 2005, demonstrate how student affairs technology shifted and changed during this time, and shape student affairs administrators' future technology use.

A Historical Perspective on Student Affairs Professionals' Use of Digital Technology

Edmund T. Cabellon, Julie Payne-Kirchmeier

The student affairs profession is at a crossroads given digital technology's historical growth and the academy's overall administrative expansion. Over the past 10 years, students, faculty, and staff have broadened engagement opportunities synchronously throughout physical and virtual spaces, utilizing mobile devices to access the Internet and a plethora of social networking services (SNS) (Kearns, 2013). With 97% of college-aged students (18–29) using digital technology tools for personal purposes, technology's professional, and educational uses became modus operandi (Duggan, 2015). During this time, faculty members experimented with technology's pedagogical merits to varying degrees of success, which unfortunately caused students, or digital natives (Prensky, 2001), to face a sense of cognitive dissonance and frustration (Burke, Marlow, & Lento, 2010; Junco, 2014). At the same time, academy leaders explored more meaningful student technology applications as these tools became increasingly pervasive (Ellison, Steinfeld, & Lampe, 2011).

Other changes have necessitated this exploration, including the academy's adoption of new, different avenues for course and program delivery, particularly through online and hybridized environments, expanding access to higher education, and evolving student demographics. In response to these changes in its student landscape, the academy has reorganized student affairs divisions into new infrastructures that support a wider range of student needs, and it has expected professional staff to adapt and take on broader responsibilities (Manning, Kinzie, & Schuh, 2013), including ones that focus on how best to support students pursuing their education in online spaces (Crawley & LeGore, 2009). Thus, student affairs administrators have catalyzed their efforts to find new ways to challenge and

NEW DIRECTIONS FOR STUDENT SERVICES, no. 155, Autumn 2016 © 2016 Wiley Periodicals, Inc.
Published online in Wiley Online Library (wileyonlinelibrary.com) • DOI: 10.1002/ss.20180

ort students through student leadership programs, enrollment and .nsition, and marketing (Ahlquist, 2015; Constantinides & Zinck Stagno, ∠011; Dare, Zapata, & Thomas, 2005; Salas & Alexander, 2008).

This chapter provides a historical perspective of student affairs professionals' use of digital and social technologies in their work on college campuses. Its purpose is to describe how these tools have evolved since 2005, demonstrate how student affairs professionals' technology use has shifted in response, and forecast their future technology use.

The Evolution of Digital and Social Technology: 2005–2015

Since 2005, the academy has been gradually adopting digital technology tools, at first primarily in its business operations and communications infrastructure (Bowen, 2013). This slow adoption matched other professions, such as the medical field; researchers cited difficulty with organizational change as the reason for its moderate pace (Clauson, Singh-Fanco, Sircar-Ramsewak, Joseph, & Sandars, 2013). Despite college students' growing demands in the digital age, higher education leaders have not generally mirrored the speed and flexibility in digital technology adoption that has been demonstrated by leaders in agriculture and business (Johnson, Adams-Becker, Estrada, & Freeman, 2014). This slow pace has not allowed higher education to keep up with rapidly changing technology, which has now redefined the time, place, and format of interaction and engagement between people (boyd, 2014; Crook, 2013). Digital technology has, in short, changed the very face of student affairs work by inserting itself without warning into the developmental and social processes of a collegiate campus environment. As such, through the Internet's evolution, the new communication model created by social networking services, and the rise of mobile smartphone adoption, higher education has fundamentally changed without the academy's collective consent (Bowen, 2013).

The Internet. The Internet's development was an offshoot of digital technology's roots in computer hardware and telecommunications tools, such as the telephone and telegraph (Ceruzzi, 2013). Its foundations were laid in the 1950s and 1960s, when personal computing technology became more reliable in real-time computing speed, allowing a machine to respond instantly to user input (Crook, 2013; Dutton, 2013). For many, it is synonymous with a program that was developed in the early 1990s called the World Wide Web (Crook, 2013), which electronically connects computers and servers to one another. This global system of networked computers, servers, and routers, which comprises the modern Internet, has transformed many aspects of society and social interaction (Ellison & boyd, 2013).

Haigh, Russell, and Dutton (2015) noted that the Internet has grown amorphous across the world, exceeding the scope of any simple definition. Communication methods expanded, providing more opportunities to connect globally (Dutton, 2013). Warschauer and Matuchniak (2010) argued that people began to consume and produce Internet content educationally more frequently. The diverse sets of practices, beliefs, and attitudes evolving around these uses has brought prominence to key related issues, including privacy, freedom of expression, and quality of information (Elton & Carey, 2013).

Over the past 10 years, the Internet's educational benefits have continued to emerge in ways not previously imagined by higher education leaders. Ebner, Lienhardt, Rohns, and Meyer (2010) noted examples, such as the in-class use of microblogs and electronic portfolios to showcase academic work for public feedback and conversation (Dalton, 2007). In addition, the academy's Internet use has increased student contact through mentorship opportunities that foster student support and development (Booth & Esposito, 2011). However, 24/7 access to classroom information, feedback, and connection has had both positive and negative implications for students, faculty, and student affairs professionals. Junco (2012) argued that student Internet use might negatively impact grades because of students' multitasking attempts. Although the Internet's educational limits have continued to be tested, its informal, process-oriented learning paradigm has provided the progressive academic experience reflected in today's online learning modalities, including massive open online courses (MOOCs) and academic engagement through social networking sites.

Social Networking Sites (SNS). *Social networking sites* is an umbrella term used to describe online, electronic communication tools, such as Facebook, Twitter, and Instagram, which allow individuals to construct profiles, display user connections, share information, and search within a list of said connections (boyd & Ellison, 2007). Over time, terms such as "social media" and "digital social networks" have expanded the SNS definition to describe the collaborative and community nature of these communication systems (Joosten, 2012). Researchers argued that disparity about a single SNS definition creates challenges to understanding its impact and scope fully (Kaplan & Haenlein, 2010).

Higher education's SNS use emerged in 2005 as the second Internet iteration took shape as "Web 2.0" (O'Reilly, 2005). Web 2.0 reflected the new social paradigm of Web-based communication, characterized as "many to many," a significant change from the former "one to one" and "one to many" communication paradigms (Shirky, 2009). This unfolding phenomenon created disparity across higher education as its leaders debated its application merits and the inevitable changes it would bring to the academy (Gismondi, 2015). Nonetheless, colleges and universities continued to explore how best to utilize these dynamic communication tools in and out of the classroom (Martinez-Alemán & Wartman, 2010).

During the past decade, educational researchers have increasingly examined topics associated with the impact of SNS on the academy and its students. Research has included the relationship between Facebook usage and social well-being (Burke et al., 2010); social tie strength and the building of social capital (Ellison et al., 2011); collaboration and teamwork (Okoro, Hausman, & Washington, 2012); and classroom use and its subsequent implications (Hung & Yuen, 2010). In addition, research on SNS topics that intersect with gender, ethnicity, and income (Junco, Merson, & Salter, 2010), retention and adjustment to college (Ward, 2010; Yang & Brown, 2013), and personality and self-esteem (Baker & Oswald, 2010; Tazghini & Siedlecki, 2013) have provided student affairs administrators and academy leaders a variety of perspectives to gain a greater understanding on students' SNS use and the impact of this use on different components of the student experience.

Although the depth and breadth of these research topics are important for higher education in general, more relevant to student affairs professionals in particular has been research on the impact of SNS on student engagement. Researchers noted that the academy's Facebook, Twitter, and Instagram use dominated a variety of student engagement experiments (Cheung, Chiu, & Lee, 2011; Junco, 2014). However, because students primarily utilized and engaged with SNS for personal reasons, faculty and staff met considerable resistance to its academic or professional possibilities (Turkle, 2011). In response, higher education leaders developed new policies, procedures, and standards to assist with SNS implementation efforts (Pasquini, 2014). Yet, as each new student class arrived with growing and evolving SNS expectations and mobile device ubiquity, higher education's inconsistent academic and co-curricular SNS adoption failed to meet these expectations, resulting in frustration for both students and the academy. This was manifested through the inconsistent ways universities implemented efforts to support students' technology use. Cabellon (2016) highlighted that ACPA and NASPA began intentionally providing professional technology development education at their respective national conferences in 2013, 2014, and 2015. In fact, in 2015 the ACPA and NASPA professional competencies were updated to include technology.

Researchers began to study Facebook use, as it became the SNS with the highest rate of use among college students (Heiberger & Harper, 2008; Junco, 2012). To date, Facebook is the largest social networking service on earth, boasting nearly 1 billion users, and its goal is to give people the power to share their lives and stay connected. Students who were engaged on Facebook integrated into the college community online and extended opportunities to connect with faculty and administrators (Heiberger & Harper, 2008). Although more studies on how first-year students use SNS is needed (Strayhorn, 2012), researchers have identified positive relationships between the number of Facebook connections a student has and their level of social adjustment to the institutional environment (Morris, Reese, Beck, & Mattis, 2010).

Additionally, educators have presented a strong case for student engagement via utilizing Twitter in and out of the classroom. As one of the top

SNS used by adults ages 18–29 (Brenner & Smith, 2013), Twitter enables its users to openly communicate online in the form of messages of 140 characters or less, called tweets (boyd & Ellison, 2007). Some faculty members and administrators began integrating Twitter into their classroom pedagogy and administrative practice because of message simplicity, something that was previously achieved only through texting (Brenner & Smith, 2013). Twitter can be used to reimagine existing classroom activities, such as note taking, class communication, and collaboration on group projects (Cronin, 2011). Additionally, as a 21st-century personal learning network (PLN), Twitter allows students to customize, complement, and enhance their educational experience (Chamberlin & Lehmann, 2011). Tess (2013) noted that, as the digital age progresses, the academy's SNS use would reflect the growing empirical evidence of SNS effectiveness.

Mobile Devices.   As Internet and SNS access and use has continued to rise, higher education faculty, staff, and students have utilized mobile smartphones as their main digital technology tool (Duggan & Smith, 2013). Marston, Blankenship, and Atkinson (2014) described the smartphone as a mobile telephone offering advanced access to Internet functionalities, such as Web site browsing and social networking. In addition, college students used smartphones, personal computers, and laptops to create and moderate content (Cabellon & Junco, 2015). In fact, these students, aged 18–29, produced more Internet content, including social networking posts, music, and videos, than any other age demographic (Junco, 2014). Although higher education leaders have slowly developed a mind-set for the smartphone's potential co-curricular uses, most of the literature has remained focused primarily on academic uses.

Gikas and Grant (2013) argued that mobile devices have the potential to replace existing digital technology tools as the primary tool for increased interaction between students and faculty. Additionally, they noted that mobile smartphones provide the ability to collaborate with fellow students. This collaboration was viewed as an added benefit, with the researchers recognizing the potential of peer-to-peer learning utilizing a tool already familiar to the student, often referred to as a "native" tool.

In addition, Matias and Wolf (2013) cited a number of ways in which students used mobile devices in their coursework. For example, collaborative learning was achieved by taking class notes using a mobile document sharing application, such as Evernote or Google Drive. Students updated, edited, and commented on the document in real time, both in and out of the classroom, and accessed the document during class for discussion or out of class for test preparation. In another example, students used a real simple syndication (RSS) application on their smartphones to collect articles, books, and news items on a particular topic for an upcoming paper. They utilized a mobile application such as Google Alerts to develop a daily digest of recently created content related to keywords that they set, thereby generating a current review of articles, stories, and blogs about their research topic. Students were leveraging the power of their mobile devices and associated SNS in a multitude of ways to enhance their educational experiences.

As mobile learning practices continued to rise in the academy, Wankel and Blessinger (2013) identified two key principles for optimized adoption. First, educational leaders viewed mobile learning environments as global communities, ones in which access to learning was not restricted by externally imposed space and time constraints; rather, flexible learning was valued and practiced by both faculty and students. Tossell, Kortum, Shepard, Rahmati, and Zhong (2015) concurred, noting that the largest barrier to full adoption of educational mobile device use was acceptance of this new student-learning paradigm, beyond classroom walls during a specific time and day. Second, educational leaders recognized that anytime and anywhere learning environments fostered a greater sense of immediacy, interactivity, and authenticity. Vazquez-Cano (2014) agreed, highlighting that learner self-efficacy and learning autonomy increased through fostered, self-regulated learning produced a diversity of learning contexts. Researchers argued that mobile devices may serve as educational gateways to broader learning opportunities that challenge contemporary students unlike ever before (Jarvela, Naykki, Laru, & Luokkanen, 2007).

Student Affairs Administrators' Digital Technology Use: 2005–2015

Throughout the new millennia, student demographic shifts and digital technology ubiquity signaled student affairs administrators' innovation attempts (Torres & Walbert, 2010). Although student learning and co-curricular experiences across the university remained of paramount focus (National Association of Student Personnel Administrators [NASPA], 2004), emerging scholarship on technology's growing impact on higher education and student affairs became more prevalent, particularly as online learning and virtual classrooms began to expand. Dare et al. (2005) argued that students in online environments had different needs than those physically present; yet, higher education's digital technology research remained primarily pedagogically focused.

Digital technology use by student affairs administrators has not been widely reflected in academic literature over the past 10 years. As more Internet generation students entered colleges with a broader technology knowledge base and mind-set, student affairs administrators' digital technology use was just beginning (Junco & Mastrodicasa, 2007). Martinez-Alemán and Wartman (2010) argued that the gap in the literature was due to a combination of technology's swift evolution and the academic publishing process's slow ability to respond to it at the same pace. Consequently, student affairs administrators who were early digital technology adopters utilized Web sites and social networks to share practitioner-based content meant to illuminate meaningful applications (Barr, McClellan, & Sandeen, 2014). More recent doctoral research focused on digital technology and highlighted emerging topics including but not limited to digital student leadership (Ahlquist, 2015), civic student engagement through social media (Gismondi, 2015), and newly admitted student interactions via Twitter use (Logan, 2015). As the use of digital technology continues to be explored in student affairs work, scholars and scholar-practitioners alike must investigate more aspects of its use and impact on the profession.

Evolution of Student Affairs Technology Perspectives.   Since 2005, student affairs technology literature has reflected a variety of perspectives as Internet, SNS, and mobile device use expanded and provided growing administrative challenges (Dare et al., 2005). These historical (Guidry, 2008), online (Moneta, 2005), and student engagement (Junco, 2014) perspectives provided an important, initial network of scholarship and documents. Hargittai (2008) asserted that broader understanding of various digital technology perspectives might unlock expanded professional and educational uses.

Guidry (2012b) argued that technology adoption has always been part of the student affairs evolution. Administrative topics such as dealing with a computer (Penn, 1976), reducing anxiety related to personal computer use (Barrow & Karris, 1985), increasing computer literacy (Bogal-Allbritten & Allbritten, 1985), developing a master's degree in student affairs information sciences (MacLean, 1986), and coordination of computer use in student affairs offices (Whyte, 1987) have been addressed within the student affairs profession over the past 30 years (as cited in Guidry, 2012a). Guidry's (2008) historical views on student affairs technology helped student affairs administrators understand the cyclical nature of technology's role in student affairs and how best to separate facts from myths. Historically, technology's applications within student affairs have evolved from simple recruitment, referral, and retention uses (Erwin & Miller, 1985) to those incorporating more engagement, development, collaboration, and educational outcomes.

Moneta (2005) suggested that student affairs' business practices would need to move online to support growing numbers of students exploring online spaces. Kruger (2005) challenged this notion through critical questions and ongoing debate about student affairs administrators' role in online learning spaces. These same questions remain relatively unanswered today (Cabellon & Junco, 2015). In addition, Dare et al. (2005) suggested that student affairs administrators also needed to assess the co-curricular needs of distance learners in order to be fully effective.

As discussed further in Chapter 5 in this volume, over the previous decade, the technology perspectives of student affairs professionals have focused primarily on student engagement through SNS (Junco, 2014). Although SNS academic literature focused on Facebook and Twitter use, student affairs–related uses have emerged, including improving student retention. Eckles and Stradley (2012) noted that students' online friends' engagement and attrition behaviors had a greater impact on retention than previously understood. Morris and others (2010) concurred, citing Facebook as a tool through which student affairs professionals could help keep students engaged with each other in an attempt to augment community-building efforts and thereby increase retention. In some ways, meaningful use of SNS has supported current changes in the student affairs profession in that student affairs professionals are considering the use of SNS and other digital technology tools as fundamental to their work with student engagement (Cabellon & Junco, 2015).

Notably, student affairs administrators who have used digital technology in their work have had to endure the challenges of change. This emergent change was built upon previous successes under exemplary leadership, an understanding of organizational culture, and the willingness to build cross-divisional relationships (Bess & Dee, 2012). In particular, student affairs administrators intentionally built partnerships with information technology colleagues for divisional project management and larger technology purchases (Cabellon, 2016). Kleinglass (2005) argued that building coalitions of support within the information technology division might garner a deeper perspective. As student affairs administrators explored additional ways to utilize digital technology to enhance existing services and programs, students became more comfortable with their own expanded uses (Grover & Stewart, 2010).

Student Affairs Administrative Use of Digital Technology.   Student affairs administrators have widely experimented with digital technology tools to augment, enhance, and improve their practice (Cabellon & Junco, 2015). As noted previously, recent literature reflected these uses, focusing on student leadership programs (Ahlquist, 2015), enrollment and transition (Salas & Alexander, 2008), and marketing (Constantinides & Zinck Stagno, 2011). Of course, as SNS tools have grown more sophisticated, more student affairs professionals have explored more ways to achieve increased student engagement (Junco, 2014).

College student leadership programs have provided meaningful co-curricular education for all involved (Elkins, 2015). Ahlquist (2015) argued that developing student leaders through digital technology was essential for supporting traditional identity development. Students accomplished this goal by reflecting on their leadership experiences through electronic portfolios, highlighted by self-created videos and graphics, as well as critical writing samples (Bresciani, 2006; Dalton, 2007). Additionally, Gismondi (2015) asserted that leadership development through digital civic engagement on SNS provided undergraduates with meaningful opportunities to create social good through social media.

These digital leadership representations have also provided enrollment services professionals in student affairs meaningful demonstrations of student success. Logan (2015) noted that focused Twitter interactions with newly admitted students increased enrollment and retention numbers by intentionally engaging them in spaces they actively occupied. Although SNS have been important, digital communication use to support retention extended beyond them to also include instant messaging on Web sites (Salas & Alexander, 2008), accessibility for students with disabilities (Korbel, McGuire, Banerjee, & Saunders, 2011), and digitally supporting students as they go through various transitions (Gray, Vitak, Easton, & Ellison, 2013). Salas and Alexander (2008) also noted the importance of utilizing these digital communication tools for student conversations in order to realize their potential for increased retention.

Despite the ubiquity of digital communication tools (Brandtzaeg, 2012), student affairs professionals primarily used them for marketing and communication (Constantinides & Zinck-Stagno, 2011; Greenhow, 2009). This was due, in part, to college students' increased mobile smartphone access and use (Smith, Rainie, & Zickuhr, 2011). Timm and Junco (2008) anticipated this movement, stating that as more students used smartphones as their primary electronic device, student affairs professionals would have to adjust student communication efforts beyond a marketing paradigm. Junco (2014) argued that increasing student engagement efforts could extend through the intersections of expanded communication paradigms, psychosocial online identity development, and evolving legal implications. In order to evolve, student affairs professionals would need to grow their digital technology acumen (Salas & Alexander, 2008).

Educational researchers and scholars have produced a plethora of meaningful scholarship about the evolution of the student affairs profession (Whitt & Schuh, 2015b) and the impact of digital technology upon the academy (Bowen, 2013). In order to grow the student affairs profession in the digital age, student affairs administrators must develop a digital technology mind-set that builds upon existing adoption and integration (Kuk, 2012). A study that analyzes how student affairs professionals have utilized digital technology in their work with students over the past 10 years may illuminate future applications.

The future of the student affairs profession remains linked to the academy's evolving digital technology use (Whitt & Schuh, 2015a). In order to support students' changing needs, student affairs professionals have considered how these technological advances impacted their work (Barr et al., 2014), such as connecting with online students (Junco, 2013; Shea, 2006), SNS engagement strategies (Ahlquist, 2015; Logan, 2015; Junco, 2014), and creating infrastructures to support these new technologies (Barr et al., 2014; Tull & Kuk, 2013). Yet, although traditional student affairs research topics such as assessment (Elkins, 2015), student learning and success (Torres & Walbert, 2010), and budget and finance (Gansemer-Topf & Englin, 2015) remain constant, the addition of technology as a formal student affairs competency illuminated its emerging foundational nature (College Student

Educators International and Student Affairs Professionals in Higher Education [ACPA & NASPA], 2015).

The Future of Student Affairs Administrators' Technology Use

As the higher education enterprise continues to shift and change, student affairs administrators must consider how their future use of technology will change to complement their evolving roles in the academy. Notably, technology's implications in college students' lives (Dare et al., 2005; Junco, 2014; Tull & Kuk, 2013), combined with new state and federal compliance mandates, have increased the complexities related to the expansion of administrative responsibilities (Dungy & Gordon, 2011). Moreover, student affairs leaders have acknowledged that these competing priorities demand more nimble responses (Manning et al., 2013; McClellan & Stringer, 2009). For many student affairs leaders, training and development on how to incorporate and utilize digital technology platforms in their work will be crucial for successfully integrating these powerful tools into the profession.

Additionally, when scanning the overall student affairs profession, Martinez-Alemán and Wartman (2010) argued that student affairs administrators' digital technology literacy level was not fluent, but cursory at best. In fact, student affairs graduate school programs have insufficiently integrated digital technology knowledge into their curricula. Furthermore, both ACPA and NASPA have provided limited professional development opportunities to help its members gain a deeper understanding (Cabellon & Junco, 2015), although both associations indicate technology as a core competency of the profession (ACPA & NASPA, 2015). This disconnect between the professed value of technology in the student affairs profession and the lack of development opportunities offered by the two leading student affairs associations is a critical gap that must be addressed if student affairs is to remain relevant in the field of higher education.

Yet, significant research highlights that student affairs administrators' digital technology use has the potential to further augment traditional in-person co-curricular student experiences (Barr et al., 2014; Elkins, 2015; Torres & Walbert, 2010). For example, Cabellon (2016) noted that between 2005 and 2015, student affairs professionals generally utilized digital technology tools to build capacity in their work, complement existing engagement opportunities, and affect the organizational change process on their own campuses and throughout the student affairs profession. Given the recent addition of technology as a new student affairs competency (ACPA & NASPA, 2015), how might student affairs professionals increase their sophistication utilizing digital technology tools in the future?

Student affairs divisional leaders should explore the creation of new positions to purposefully engage online and hybrid students, as well as to lead divisional technology efforts to fully incorporate digital technology into practice. In addition, as the use of mobile technology becomes ubiquitous, student affairs educators must match faculty's innovative uses (Matias & Wolf, 2013). The size, scope, and resources available for different student affairs divisions will dictate how feasible it would be to add positions or expand an existing position's scope to address digital technology's full implementation. Strategic, cross-divisional partnerships would be another way to expand a student affairs division's desire to expand their digital technology implementation plans.

Next, ACPA and NASPA should work closely together to lead the profession's exploration of digital technology use, utilizing the new technology competency (ACPA & NASPA,2015) to galvanize professional development and update graduate preparation programs. This process will be challenging, given the foundational literature of student affairs' education, which reflects counseling, administration, and student development theory (Torres & Walbert, 2010). In addition, although recent changes to student affairs graduate programs reflect the inclusion of social justice education and building specific skills, including budgeting, grant writing, supervision, and online delivery methods through learning management systems (Ortiz et al., 2015), there has been no clear systematic change. Although the associations have included digital technology as part of the student affairs profession's core competencies (ACPA & NASPA,2015), meaningful change might not be actualized until significant additions to student affairs graduate curricula have been made.

Finally, student affairs educators might explore more ways to infuse digital technology tools throughout their existing programs and services. A place to begin is in grounding efforts in existing digital technology literature, focused on topics such as student leadership (Ahlquist, 2015), using electronic portfolios as reflective tools (Bresciani, 2006; Dalton, 2007), or civic engagement (Gismondi, 2015). Cabellon (2016) stresses that student affairs administrators should then include the following questions as part of their planning process:

1. How do we deliver this program or service in a digital format, and what type of data could we gain?
2. How do we utilize digital communication platforms to share our division's learning outcomes?
3. How do we connect the data we collect to the university's central student information system?
4. How do we reallocate budgetary resources to support our departmental use of digital technology tools to inspire innovative practice?

With each successful digital technology implementation, practitioners are collecting, analyzing, utilizing, and sharing data that might help inform future student affairs practice (Wishon & Rome, 2012).

Conclusion

Student affairs administrators have only begun to discover digital technology's educational and professional potential (Guidry, 2012b). Student affairs professional associations, senior student affairs officers, and student affairs administrators are all equally responsible for discovering new technological applications that might expand their roles within the academy and its ongoing online adoption. Although the residential experience remains fundamental in higher education, given shifting demographics in higher education, university leaders must purposefully find ways to support commuter, hybrid, and online students equally. Given its anytime, anywhere communication capabilities, digital technology enables student affairs administrators to engage geographically distant students and connect them to the university community. The complexity, size, and type of each institution must be taken into account as part of any meaningful implementation, as one single approach will not fit all.

References

Ahlquist, J. (2015). *Developing digital student leaders: A mixed methods study of student leadership, identity and decision making on social media* (Doctoral dissertation). Retrieved from ProQuest Dissertations and Theses. (Accession No. 3713711).

Baker, L. R., & Oswald, D. L. (2010). Shyness and online social networking services. *Journal of Social and Personal Relationships, 27*(7), 873–889.

Barr, M. J., McClellan, G. S., & Sandeen, A. (2014). *Making change happen in student affairs*. New York, NY: Wiley.

Barrow, B. R., & Karris, P. M. (1985). A hands-on workshop for reducing computer anxiety. *Journal of College Student Personnel, 26*(2), 167–168.

Bess, J. L., & Dee, J. R. (2012). *Understanding college and university organization: Theories for effective policy and practice*(Vol. 2). Sterling, VA: Stylus.

Bogal-Allbritten, R., & Allbritten, B. (1985). A computer literacy course for students and professionals in human services. *Journal of College Student Personnel, 26*(2), 170–171.

Booth, M., & Esposito, A. (2011). Mentoring 2.0—High tech/high touch approaches foster student support and development in higher education. In L. A. Wankel & C. Wankel (Eds.), *Higher education administration with social media. Cutting-edge technologies in higher education* (Volume 2, pp. 85–103). Bingley, UK: Emerald Group Publishing Limited.

Bowen, W. G. (2013). *Higher education in the digital age*. Princeton, NJ: Princeton University Press.

boyd, d. (2014). *It's complicated: The social lives of networked teens*. New Haven, CT: Yale University Press.

boyd, d. m., & Ellison, N. B. (2007). Social networking sites: Definition, history, and scholarship. *Journal of Computer-Mediated Communication, 13*(1), 210–230.

Brandtzaeg, P. B. (2012). Social networking sites: Their users and social implications—a longitudinal study. *Journal of Computer-Mediated Communication, 17*(4), 467–488.

Brenner, J., & Smith, A. (2013, August 5). 72% of online adults are social networking site users. Retrieved from http://www.pewinternet.org/Reports/2013/social-networking-sites.aspx

Bresciani, M. J. (2006). Electronic co-curricular student portfolios: Putting them into practice. In K. Kruger (Ed.), *Technology in student affairs: Supporting student learning and services* (pp. 69–76). San Francisco, CA: Jossey-Bass.

Burke, M., Marlow, C., & Lento, T. (2010). Social networking activity and social well-being. Paper presented at the CHI 2010 Proceedings of the SIGCHI Conference on Human Factors in Computing Systems, Atlanta, GA. Retrieved from http://dl.acm.org/citation.cfm?id=1753613

Cabellon, E. T. (2016). *Redefining student affairs through digital technology: A ten-year historiography of digital technology use by student affairs administrators* (Doctoral dissertation). Retrieved from ProQuest Dissertations and Theses. (Accession No. 10013238).

Cabellon, E. T., & Junco, R. (2015). The digital age of student affairs. *New Directions for Student Services, 151,* 49–61.

Ceruzzi, P. (2013). The historical context. In S. Price, C. Jewitt, & B. Brown (Eds.), *The SAGE handbook of digital technology research (pp.* 9–25). Thousand Oaks, CA: Sage.

Chamberlin, L., & Lehmann, K. (2011). Twitter in higher education. In C. Wankel (Ed.), *Educating educators with social media* (pp. 375–391). Bingley, UK: Emerald Group Publishing.

Cheung, C. M. K., Chiu, P., & Lee, M. K. O. (2011). Online social networks: Why do students use Facebook? *Computers in Human Behavior, 27*(4), 1337–1343.

Clauson, K. A., Singh-Franco, D., Sircar-Ramsewak, F., Joseph, S., & Sandars, J. (2013). Social media use and educational preferences among first-year pharmacy students. *Teaching and Learning in Medicine, 25*(2), 122–128.

College Student Educators International (ACPA) & National Association of Student Personnel Administrators (NASPA). (2015). Professional competency areas for student affairs educators. Retrieved from http://www.naspa.org/images/uploads/main/ACPA_NASPA_Professional_Competencies_FINAL.pdf

Constantinides, E., & Zinck Stagno, M. C. (2011). Potential of the social media as instruments of higher education marketing: a segmentation study. *Journal of Marketing for Higher Education, 21*(1), 7–24.

Crawley, A., & LeGore, C. (2009). Supporting online students. In G. S. McClellan & J. Stringer (Eds.), *The handbook of student affairs administration* (pp. 288–308). San Francisco, CA: Jossey-Bass.

Cronin, J. J. (2011). The classroom as a virtual community: An experience with student backchannel discourse. *Business Education Innovation Journal, 3*(2), 56–65.

Crook, C. (2013). The field of digital technology research. In S. Price, C. Jewitt, & B. Brown (Eds.), *The SAGE handbook of digital technology research* (pp. 26–40). Thousand Oaks, CA: Sage.

Dalton, J. C. (2007). Concluding observations and implications of e-portfolios for student affairs leadership and programming. *New Directions for Student Services, 119,* 99–106.

Dare, L. A., Zapata, L. P., & Thomas, A. G. (2005). Assessing the needs of distance learners: A student affairs perspective. In K. Kruger (Ed.), *Technology in student affairs: Supporting student learning and services* (pp. 39–54). San Francisco, CA: Jossey-Bass.

Duggan, M. (2015, August 19). Mobile messaging and social media 2015. Retrieved from http://www.pewinternet.org/2015/08/19mobile-messaging-and-social-media-2015/

Duggan, M., & Smith, A. (2013, December 30). Social media update 2013. Retrieved from http://www.pewinternet.org/2013/12/30/social-media-update-2013/

Dungy, G., & Gordon, S. A. (2011). The development of student affairs. In J. H. Schuh, S. R. Jones, & S. R. Harper (Eds.), *Student services: A handbook for the profession* (5th ed., pp. 61–80). San Francisco, CA: Jossey-Bass.

Dutton, W. H. (2013). Internet studies: The foundations of a transformative field. In W. Dutton (Ed.), *The Oxford handbook of Internet studies* (pp. 14–49). Oxford, UK: Oxford University Press.

Ebner, M., Lienhardt, C., Rohs, M., & Meyer, I. (2010). Microblogs in higher education—A chance to facilitate informal and process-oriented learning? *Computers & Education, 55*(1), 92–100.

Eckles, J. E., & Stradley, E. G. (2012). A social network analysis of student retention using archival data. *Social Psychology of Education, 15*(2), 165–180.

Elkins, B. (2015). Looking back and ahead: What we must learn from 30 years of student affairs assessment. *New Directions for Student Services, 151,* 39–48.

Ellison, N. B., & boyd, d. (2013). Sociality through social network sites. In W. Dutton (Ed.), *The Oxford handbook of Internet studies* (pp. 151–172). Oxford, UK: Oxford University Press.

Ellison, N. B., Steinfeld, C., & Lampe, C. (2011). Connection strategies: Social capital implications of Facebook-enabled communication practices. *New Media & Society, 13*(6), 873–892.

Elton, M. C. J., & Carey, J. (2013). The prehistory or the Internet and its traces in the present: Implications for defining the field. In W. Dutton (Ed.), *The Oxford handbook of Internet studies* (pp. 51–92). Oxford, UK: Oxford University Press.

Erwin, T. D., & Miller, S. W. (1985). Technology and the three Rs. *NASPA Journal, 22*(4), 47–51.

Gansemer-Topf, A. M., & Englin, P. D. (2015). Contemporary challenges in student affairs budgeting and finance. *New Directions for Student Services, 151,* 63–78.

Gikas, J., & Grant, M. M. (2013). Mobile computing devices in higher education: Student perspectives on learning with cellphones, devices, & social media. *Internet & Higher Education, 19,* 18–26.

Gismondi, A. (2015). *#CivicEngagement: An exploratory study of social media use and civic engagement among undergraduates* (Doctoral dissertation). Retrieved from ProQuest Dissertations and Theses database. (UMI Accession No. 3688220).

Gray, R., Vitak, J., Easton, E. W., & Ellison, N. B. (2013). Examining social adjustment to college in the age of social media: Factors influencing successful transitions and persistence. *Computers & Education, 67,* 193–207.

Greenhow, C. (2009). Tapping the wealth of social networks for professional development. *Learning & Leading with Technology, 36*(8), 10–11.

Grover, A., & Stewart, D. W. (2010). Defining interactive social media in an educational context. In C. Wankel (Ed.), *Cutting edge social media approaches to business education: Teaching with LinkedIn, Facebook, Twitter, Second Life, and blogs* (pp. 7–38). Charlotte, NC: Information Age Publishing.

Guidry, K. R. (2008). Exploding a myth: Student affairs' historical relationship with technology. *eJournal, 9*(2). Retrieved from http://studentaffairs.com/ejournal/Summer_2008/ExplodingaMyth.html

Guidry, K. R. (2012a, April 3). When did student affairs begin discussing technology as competency? [Web log post]. Retrieved from http://mistakengoal.com/blog/2012/04/03/when-did-student-affairs-begin-discussing-technology-as-a-competency/

Guidry, K. R. (2012b, June 22). Ongoing research into student affairs technology history [Web log post]. Retrieved from http://mistakengoal.com/blog/2012/06/22/ongoing-research-into-student-affairs-technology-history/

Haigh, T., Russell, A. L., & Dutton, W. H. (2015). Histories of the Internet. *Information & Culture, 50*(2), 143–159.

Hargittai, E. (2008). Whose space? Differences among users and non-users of social network sites. *Journal of Computer Mediated Communication, 13*(1), 276–297.

Heiberger, G., & Harper, R. (2008). Have you Facebooked Astin lately? Using technology to increase student involvement. *New Directions for Student Services, 124,* (19–35). San Francisco, CA: Jossey-Bass.

Hung, H., & Yuen, S. (2010). Educational use of social networking technology in higher education. *Teaching in Higher Education, 15*(6), 703–714.

Jarvela, S., Naykki, P., Laru, J., & Luokkanen, T. (2007). Structuring and regulating collaborative learning in higher education with wireless and mobile tools. *Journal of Educational Technology & Society, 10*(4), 71–79.

Johnson, L., Adams-Becker, S., Estrada, V., & Freeman, A. (2014). *NMC horizon report: 2014 higher education edition.* Austin, TX: New Media Consortium.

Joosten, T. (2012). *Social media for educators: Strategies and best practices.* New York, NY: Wiley.

Junco, R. (2012). In-class multitasking and academic performance. *Computers in Human Behavior, 28*(6), 2236–2243.

Junco, R. (2014). *Engaging students through social media: Evidence-based practices for use in student affairs.* San Francisco, CA: Jossey-Bass.

Junco, R., & Mastrodicasa, J. (2007). *Connecting to the net generation: What higher education professionals need to know about today's students.* Washington, DC: NASPA.

Junco, R., Merson, D., & Salter, D. W. (2010). The effect of gender, ethnicity, and income on college students' use of communication technologies. *Cyberpsychology, Behavior, and Social Networking, 13*(6), 619–627.

Kaplan, A. M., & Haenlein, M. (2010). Users of the world, unite! The challenges and opportunities of social media. *Business Horizons, 53*(1), 59–68.

Kearns, S. (2013). *First-year college students' perceptions of their experiences using information and communication technologies in higher education* (Doctoral dissertation). Retrieved from ProQuest Dissertations and Theses database. (UMI Accession No. 3567288).

Kleinglass, N. (2005). Who is driving the changing landscape in student affairs? In K. Kruger (Ed.), *Technology in student affairs: Supporting student learning and services* (pp. 25–38). San Francisco, CA: Jossey-Bass.

Korbel, D. M., McGuire, J. M., Banerjee, M., & Saunders, S. (2011). Transition strategies to ensure active student engagement. *New Directions for Student Services, 134,* 35–46.

Kruger, K. (2005). What we know and the difference it makes. *New Directions for Student Services, 112,* 103–107.

Kuk, L. (2012). The changing nature of student affairs. In A. Tull & L. Kuk (Eds.), *New realities in the management of student affairs* (pp. 3–12). Sterling, VA: Stylus.

Logan, T. J. (2015). *An investigation of Twitter interactions amongst newly admitted college students at a large public institution.* (Unpublished doctoral dissertation). University of Florida, Gainesville, FL.

MacLean, L. S. (1986). Developing MIS in student affairs. *NASPA Journal, 23*(3), 2–7.

Manning, K., Kinzie, J., & Schuh, J. H. (2013). *One size does not fit all: Traditional and innovative models of student affairs practice.* New York, NY: Routledge.

Martinez-Alemán, A. M., & Wartman, K. L. (2010). Student technology use and student affairs practice. In J. Schuh, S. Jones, & S. Harper (Eds.), *Student services: A handbook for the profession* (pp. 515–534). San Francisco, CA: Jossey-Bass.

Marston, S., Blankenship, R. J., & Atkinson, J. K. (2014). How are smartphones used in higher education? *Academy of Business Research Journal, 3,* 10–27.

Matias, A., & Wolf, D. F. (2013). Engaging students in online courses through the use of mobile technology. In L. Wankel & P. Blessinger (Eds.), *Increasing engagement retention using mobile applications: Devices, Skype and texting technologies* (pp. 115–144). Bingley, UK: Emerald Group Publishing.

McClellan, G. S., & Stringer, J. (2009). *The handbook of student affairs administration.* San Francisco, CA: Jossey-Bass.

Moneta, L. (2005). Technology and student affairs: Redux. In K. Kruger (Ed.), *Technology in student affairs: Supporting student learning and services* (pp. 3–14). San Francisco, CA: Jossey-Bass.

Morris, J., Reese, J., Beck, R., & Mattis, C. (2010). Facebook usage as a predictor of retention at a private 4-year institution. *Journal of College Student Retention, 11*(3), 311–322.

National Association of Student Personnel Administrators (NASPA). (2004). Learning reconsidered: A campus-wide focus on the student experience. Retrieved from https://www.naspa.org/images/uploads/main/Learning_Reconsidered_Report. pdf

Okoro, E. A., Hausman, A., & Washington, M. C. (2012). Social media and networking technologies: An analysis of collaborative work and team communication. *Contemporary Issues in Education Research, 5*(4), 295–300.

O'Reilly, T. (2005, August 30). What is Web 2.0: Design patterns and business models for the next generation. Retrieved from http://www.oreilly.com/pub/a/web2/archive/what-is-web-20.html

Ortiz, A. M., Filimon, I., & Cole-Jackson, M. (2015). Preparing student affairs educators. *New Directions for Student Services, 151*, 78–89.

Pasquini, L. A. (2014). *Organizational identity and community values: Determining meaning in post-secondary education social media guideline and policy documents* (Doctoral dissertation). Retrieved from ProQuest Dissertations and Theses. (UMI Accession No. 1724111999).

Penn, J. R. (1976). Dealing with the computer. *NASPA Journal, 14*(2), 56–58.

Prensky, M. (2001). Digital natives, digital immigrants part 1. *On the Horizon, 9*(5), 1–6.

Salas, G., & Alexander, J. S. (2008). Technology for institutional enrollment, communication, and student success. In R. Junco & D. Timm (Eds.), *Using emerging technologies to enhance student engagement* (pp. 103–116). San Francisco, CA: Jossey-Bass.

Shea, P. A. (2006). Serving students online: Enhancing their learning experience. *New Directions for Student Services, 112*, 13–24.

Shirky, C. (2009). *Here comes everybody: The power of organizing without organizations.* New York, NY: Penguin.

Smith, A., Rainie, L., & Zickuhr, K. (2011). College students and technology. Retrieved from http://www.pewinternet.org/Reports/2011/College-students-and-technology/Report.aspx

Strayhorn, T. L. (2012). *College students' sense of belonging: A key to educational success for all students.* New York, NY: Routledge.

Tazghini, S., & Siedlecki, K. L. (2013). A mixed method approach to examining Facebook use and its relationship to self-esteem. *Computers in Human Behavior, 29*(3), 827–832.

Tess, P. A. (2013). The role of social media in higher education classes (real and virtual)—A literature review. *Computers in Human Behavior, 29*(5), A60–A68.

Timm, D., & Junco, R. (2008). Beyond the horizon. In R. Junco & D. Timm (Eds.), *Using emerging technologies to enhance student engagement* (pp. 117–125). San Francisco, CA: Jossey-Bass.

Torres, V., & Walbert, J. (2010). Envisioning the future of student affairs. Retrieved from https://www.naspa.org/images/uploads/main/Task_Force_Student_Affairs_2010_Report.pdf

Tossell, C. C., Kortum, P., Shepard, C., Rahmati, A., & Zhong, L. (2015). You can lead a horse to water but you cannot make him learn: Smartphone use in higher education. *British Journal of Educational Technology, 46*(4), 713–724.

Tull, A., & Kuk, L. (2013). *New realities in the management of student affairs.* Sterling, VA: Stylus.

Turkle, S. (2011). *Alone together: Why we expect more from technology and less from each other.* New York, NY: Basic Books.

Vazquez-Cano, E. (2014). Mobile distance learning with devices and apps in higher education. *Educational Sciences: Theory & Practice, 14*(5), 1505–1520.

Wankel, L. A., & Blessinger, P. (2013). New pathways in higher education: An introduction to using mobile technologies. In L. Wankel & P. Blessinger (Eds.), *Increasing engagement and retention using mobile applications: Devices, Skype and texting technologies* (pp. 3–18). Bingley, UK: Emerald Group Publishing.

Ward, T. H. (2010). *Social network site use and student retention at a four-year private university* (Doctoral dissertation). Retrieved from ProQuest Dissertation Database. (UMI Accession No. 3445786).

Warschauer, M., & Matuchniak, T. (2010). New technology and digital worlds: Analyzing evidence of equity in access, use, and outcomes. *Review of Research in Education, 34*(1), 179–225.

Whitt, E. J., & Schuh, J. H. (2015a). Peering into the future. *New Directions for Student Services, 151,* 89–99.

Whitt, E. J., & Schuh, J. H. (2015b). Glancing back at New Directions for Student Services, 1997–2014. *New Directions for Student Services, 151,* 3–14.

Whyte, C. B. (1987). Coordination of computer use in student affairs offices: A national update. *Journal of College Student Personnel, 28*(1), 84–86.

Wishon, G. D., & Rome, J. (2012, August 13). Enabling a data-driven university. EDUCAUSE Review. Retrieved from http://www.educause.edu/ero/article/enabling-data-driven-university

Yang, C. C., & Brown, B. B. (2013). Motives for using Facebook, patterns of Facebook activities, and late adolescents' social adjustment to college. *Journal of Youth and Adolescence, 42*(3), 403–416.

EDMUND T. CABELLON is assistant to the vice president of student affairs and enrollment management at Bridgewater State University and the former co-chair of ACPA's Presidential Task Force on Digital Technology.

JULIE PAYNE-KIRCHMEIER is associate vice president of student affairs and chief of staff at Northwestern University and is an active leader on ACPA's presidential task force on digital technology.

NEW DIRECTIONS FOR STUDENT SERVICES • DOI: 10.1002/ss

2

This chapter highlights opportunities in the digital space for student affairs professionals. A blended approach, grounded in the new technology competency recently added in the ACPA and NASPA student affairs professional competencies, is proposed for student affairs professionals' digital identity development. It includes the awareness of one's digital identity, formation of a digital decision-making model, and utilization of personal learning networks.

The Digital Identity of Student Affairs Professionals

Josie Ahlquist

"My personal identity is integrated into my professional identity. There is only one me, including on social media. It's hard enough keeping track of the one." Senior Vice Chancellor of Student Affairs, research participant at a Midwest public institution.

The quote above was captured from a recent study of 16 student affairs professionals that found that Twitter could be integrated into a holistic model of a digital identity, specifically in a leadership role in student affairs (Ahlquist, 2016). This model approached the use of technology through a value-added, philosophical lens, such as a priority to interact with students, care for their campus community, and being authentic and real online. At this chapter's core is the awareness, cultivation, and celebration of a digital identity as a student affairs professional.

Digital identity is the self-presentation method one displays online, in both personal and professional contexts. Self-presentation is "the conscious or unconscious process by which people try to influence the perception of their image, typically through social interactions" (Junco, 2014, p. 111). For student affairs professionals, these social interactions occur with both colleagues and students. A model for developing a professional identity blended with a holistic digital presence, as well as work on self that includes unpacking perceptions, self-presentation, and even performance in the digital space, is introduced in this chapter.

NEW DIRECTIONS FOR STUDENT SERVICES, no. 155, Autumn 2016 © 2016 Wiley Periodicals, Inc.
Published online in Wiley Online Library (wileyonlinelibrary.com) • DOI: 10.1002/ss.20181

This chapter uses a blended approach to digital identity, built from the College Student Educators International (ACPA) and National Association of Student Personnel Administrators (NASPA) student affairs technology (tech) competency, a student affairs digital decision-making model, and resources for personal learning networks. The tech competency was introduced in 2015, and its definition includes, ". . . the use of digital tools, resources, and technologies for the advancement of student learning, development, and success, as well as the improved performance of student affairs professionals" (ACPA & NASPA, 2015, p. 15). Therefore, recognizing and utilizing technology in their work with and for students is no longer optional for student affairs professionals—it is a requirement. Their work, especially with social media tools, begins with digital identity, which is composed of both user-generated online content and information that others post about that user. Collectively, this content is searchable through computer media tools like Google, Bing, Facebook, and more. The development of a digital identity includes the awareness of this digital content and the ongoing cultivation of content that fully represents self and improvement of self and others.

The challenge of exploring and developing a digital identity, or embracing technology tools like social media in student affairs, is keeping up with its rapid change and overcoming and changing negative perceptions of it. Digital and social technologies are quickly transforming our global society, but institutions of higher education typically move at a slower pace. At the same time, stories about social media being used to threaten or deceive others flood the news. The development of a digital identity should not be curtailed because of these challenges, but it should start with an awareness that sometimes more is going on behind the screen. Therefore, the purpose of this chapter is to explore the digital identity of student affairs professionals through the changing perceptions of technology, the impact of the student affairs technology competency, and a holistic approach to a digital identity in student affairs.

Foregoing Fear of Technology and Embracing Digital Identity Education

Social networking tools have been available for over a decade, meaning today's college students have utilized social media communication tools since they were in middle school (boyd, 2014). For student affairs professionals, the adoption of these tools started at later points in life, varying from graduate school to advanced career levels. Earlier technology adopters might have experimented with Myspace, AIM, or Yahoo messenger, then migrated to newer tools like LinkedIn, Facebook, or Instagram; however, later technology adopters likely did not use the first wave of social media tools at all. Regardless, throughout this entire time, little education has been provided

NEW DIRECTIONS FOR STUDENT SERVICES • DOI: 10.1002/ss

to guide their usage. As a result, digital identity and behavior have been a by-product of trial and error (Ahlquist, 2015; Cabellon, 2016).

The absence of training and experience for campus leaders has allowed worst-case stories to dominate their perception of social media. Mentioning applications like Yik Yak or online confession pages evokes immediate, sometimes apprehensive reactions from many college administrators. These social media sites have been used by students not only to post racist or misogynistic comments about other members of the campus community anonymously, but also to propose acts of mass violence, like a rape at Kenyon College or mass shootings at Drake University, Emory University, and the University of Central Oklahoma (Mahler, 2015). The media fuel these concerns, as TV shows like NBC's *To Catch a Predator* (Keller, 2004) and MTV's *Catfish* (Metzler & Smerling, 2012) produce real examples of the dark side of technology: how a false digital identity can hide deceptive or criminal intentions. Fear inspired by these reports has had a trickle-down effect that dampens enthusiasm for engaging with social media, embracing digital identity, and building online communities.

The use of social media by youth in particular has been viewed with apprehension by society. Boyd (2014) followed the use of social media by 166 teens over 3 years, and she overwhelmingly found that they sought out tools like social media for relationships with their peers, even though fearful parents and teachers used many conflicting and confrontational tactics to dissuade them. Challenging society's perceptions, what boyd labels "fear mongering," was behind why youth were drawn to or actually active on social media tools. Another prominent researcher, Junco (2014), also found that social media use by college students was seen in a negative light. Rather than fear, he defined this view as an adult normative perspective, "what is appropriate based upon their [adults] own expectations and norms; these expectations are no doubt influenced by popular media portrayals of social media as detrimental to youth development" (p. 96). However, if student affairs professionals adopt either of these views, fear or an adult normative perspective, they will not be able explore their own digital identity, nor will they be able to educate students about its development process.

In the past 5 years, leaders in the field of student affairs have been challenging these perceptions and encouraging their colleagues to embrace their digital identities. Cabellon (2011, paragraph 6) offered guidance to professionals working with college students, stating, "As more of our students live their lives online, we need to be intentional in our conversations, strengthen our own online identities, and help them think through their online decisions that have real world implications." An Inside Higher Ed blogger also discussed digital identity, writing, "The manner in which we engage, share, promote, and present ourselves online has become a major facet in many of our lives. No longer seen as being separate from 'real life,' an individual's digital identity is intricately connected to their overall identity" (Stoller, 2012, paragraph 2).

In the field of higher education, digital identity has also been discussed as professional digital branding reputation. In the text *Making Change Happen in Student Affairs*, Barr, McClellan, and Sandeen (2014) argued that "personal branding is about packaging one's knowledge, skills and professional experience for the purposes of promoting one's reputation and career" (p. 87). The authors connected mindfulness of personal brand as a student affairs professional with helping students be aware of their own personal brand.

Student affairs professionals need to explore their digital presence on social media platforms to become knowledgeable about the development process and understand how they connect it back to students. However, embracing a student affairs digital identity is not as simple as signing up for LinkedIn, Twitter, and Instagram. Cabellon and Junco (2015) shared, "The digital age is more than the adoption and integration of technology and communication tools. It requires those seeking to engage college students to develop the mindset, fluency, and skill necessary to add value and relevance to the contemporary college experience" (p. 3). Therefore, the remainder of this chapter discusses tools that will help professionals to develop a digital identity with the use of the student affairs tech competency, a digital decision-making model, and personal learning networks.

Technology Awareness no Longer a Choice: The Student Affairs Technology Competency

In August 2015, ACPA and NASPA released the second version of the professional competency areas for student affairs practitioners. This tool is a resource for the field, especially in developing curricula, professional development opportunities, and job descriptions. The revised competencies were the result of a collaborative gathering of both NASPA and ACPA representatives who made up the Professional Competencies task force. The task force unpacked the relevancy of the first version of the competencies, which was developed in 2010, and considered changes after 5 years in practice. A major change was the addition of a standalone technology (tech) competency, which previously was defined as a thread among all the competencies. The tech competency is described as follows:

> Focuses on the use of digital tools, resources, and technologies for the advancement of student learning, development, and success as well as the improved performance of student affairs professionals. Included within this area are knowledge, skills, and dispositions that lead to the generation of digital literacy and digital citizenship within communities of students, student affairs professionals, faculty members, and colleges and universities as a whole. (ACPA & NASPA, 2015, p. 15)

NEW DIRECTIONS FOR STUDENT SERVICES • DOI: 10.1002/ss

With the approval and implementation of the tech competency, student affairs educators no longer have a choice about whether to explore, educate, and advance technology. It is now a professional requirement.

Each competency includes three levels: foundational, intermediate, and advanced. Using the competencies as a framework, professional growth demonstrates "application, to facilitation, to leadership" (p. 15). Further professional development with technology at the intermediate and advanced level, "involve(s) a higher degree of innovativeness in the use of technology to engage students and others in learning processes" (p. 33). Each of the levels in the tech competency has 11–14 outcomes, and this chapter focuses on 3 that will guide a professional student affairs digital identity: technology adaptability, personal learning networks, and digital identity.

Technology Adaptability. The development of a digital identity needs to include an awareness of quickly evolving technologies. This includes accepting, adapting, and even embracing that technology can be remixed before you, your institution or department may be ready. The tech competency guides those exploring at the foundational level and directs professionals to, "Demonstrate adaptability in the face of fast-paced technological change" (ACPA & NASPA, 2015, p. 33). At the foundational level, professionals must be aware of adoption patterns of students and professionals, including how those tools function. Adapting to technology at a foundational level makes student affairs professionals like digital explorers, seeking out information and understanding of tools. As discussed earlier, by unpacking technology perceptions, a professional can then consider their presence and purpose in the digital space, including their digital identity.

Much can be learned from the stories of other student affairs professionals, who began to explore and flourish using technology, such as Twitter. Patrick Love, senior vice president of student affairs at New York Institute of Technology, shared his digital exploration of technology as akin to developing the courage to wade into a fast-flowing river.

When I was first introduced to Twitter it was like standing on the side of a river looking at it. I was trying to figure out how to use Twitter as a professional tool, by observing from the sideline. I didn't get it. Colleagues continued to encourage me to use it, so I went to the bank of the river and dipped my hands in, scooping the water. I got a sense of what it could do, but still didn't fully engage. Finally, after coffee with Tony Doody between Christmas and New Year's in 2012, we decided to use social media to promote our blog. I dove into the river and it completely changed my view of the tool. Being in the river helped me immediately see how useful it could be in promoting professional development. (P. Love, personal communication, August 15, 2015)

Love began by observing technology while still doubtful but relied on others to aid his adoption. In this case, Love is at the foundational level, but his colleague, Doody, displayed adaptability skills, which identifies him as being at the intermediate level. At this level, a student affairs professional should, "Model and promote adaptability among students, colleagues, and educational stakeholders in the face of fast-paced technological change and demonstrate openness to the introduction of new digital tools by others" (ACPA & NASPA, 2015, p. 34). The major shift at the intermediate level is taking on a digital educator role.

At the advanced level, one would, "Anticipate technological change and allocate personal, departmental, and/or institutional resources to foster in others dispositions of adaptability, flexibility, and openness to technological innovation" (ACPA & NASPA, 2015, p. 35). This level of influence in resource allocation can have a significant impact throughout an organization. An example at the advanced level of this outcome comes from the University of Northern Colorado, where Matthew Brinton and Colleen Sonnentag created curriculum for the Higher Education Student Affairs Leadership masters program. The program saw the need to include a course called Technology in Higher Education that addresses topics, such as social media, educational technology, and information management platforms in student affairs practice. The mission of the class includes the organizers' perspective on technology,

> It is our belief that technology is a tool to achieve learning outcomes, rather than a learning outcome in its own right. The effective integration of technology into practice has the opportunity to enhance learning and create efficiencies. However, we are not advocating for the adoption of any and all technologies for the sake of trendsetting. Rather, it is our goal that through participation in this course, students will be able to evaluate multiple technologies and think critically about their implementation in meaningful ways. (M. Brinton & C. Sonnentag, personal communication, June 15, 2015)

At this advanced level of the tech competency, an outcome such as this course provides each student in the program with technology adaptability skills. The course is structured to respond to changing trends and prioritizes the evaluation and meaning making of technology. The integration of technology into practice also includes the recognition and cultivation of a professional digital identity. Three weeks of the 15-week curriculum includes content on digital reputation and identity, and in week 14, students explore concepts of digital leadership in higher education. In turn, the digital identity education of student affairs professionals needs to include adapting to technology and working through personal perceptions, adoption, and leadership.

Digital Identity. Each level of the technology competency includes digital identity skills. Both NASPA and ACPA define digital identity as a priority for all practitioners, no matter what their role on campus is. At the foundational level, digital explorers, "demonstrate awareness of one's digital identity and engage students in learning activities related to responsible digital communications and virtual community engagement as related to their digital reputation and identity" (ACPA & NASPA, 2015, p. 33). At the intermediate level, digital educators "proactively cultivate a digital identity, presence, and reputation for one's self and by students that models appropriate online behavior and positive engagement with others in virtual communities" (p. 34). At the advanced level, professionals should provide training and leadership on the "cultivation of a genuine digital identity, presence, and reputation that models appropriate online behavior and enables open access and engagement with virtual communities as appropriate" (p. 34). Later in this chapter, recent research on student affairs leaders will define what exactly a genuine digital identity looks like. The journey of digital identity moves a practitioner from exploring and cultivating digital identity of self to educating others on digital identity, then to exemplifying digital leadership and role modeling. This continuum is already observed in the field.

Marci Walton, associate director of residence life at Xavier University, strategically developed her digital identity through foundational and intermediate outcomes utilizing student affairs personal learning networks on Twitter and Facebook. She took these skills into an advanced level for her staff while working at Loyola University Chicago.

> Several times in my first year as a mid-level professional, I offered a professional development space that got new professionals, graduate students, and other mid-level pros in my department in the same space. They brought devices or computers while I showed a live feed of #SAchat. Together, we engaged in professional development both in person and online, and in this case, it happened simultaneously . . . Digital engagement is wonderful, but we are doing our new professionals a disservice if we are unwilling to teach digital engagement as a skill, much like we teach duty response, advising structures, or supervising student teams. (M. Walton, personal communication, July 25, 2015)

Utilizing advanced outcomes of the technology competency does not need to be costly; many times, at least one person finding time to offer creative programming and space can have a significant impact. However, it is not as simple as telling students or colleagues to just get into technology. As Walton shared, "We often tell new professionals, 'Get on Twitter! The networking is great!' but then never help them with making meaning of the online space. This meaning making is where conversations of digital identity come to life" (personal communication, July 25, 2015).

The advanced-level outcome calls for a genuine digital identity, presenting a significant shift in the role of professionals in student affairs as digital identity educators. The advanced level also includes digital role modeling leadership language, which the field of student affairs has never used before. In the next section of this chapter, I outline a holistic model related to the tech competency that student affairs professionals can integrate into their professional growth. This model enables educators to embrace a genuine digital identity in both their personal and professional worlds.

A Holistic Perspective of Digital Identity in Student Affairs

At the time of this publication, limited scholarly research guiding student affairs professionals' digital identity development exists. Cabellon and Junco (2015) pointed to the discrepancy in research as well as practice, "Student affairs professionals are ill equipped to meet students where they are on social media, relegating these sites to minor roles in their own professional competency portfolios" (p. 3). These researchers believe this does harm, including "a lack of understanding of the full experience of our students" (p. 3). As a social media researcher, I saw this gap years ago and sought to explain the usage of social communication tools among a group of senior leaders in student affairs (Ahlquist, 2016). As a result, my research proposes the use of social media as a personal yet strategic approach for digital identity, relationship building, and digital leadership in student affairs.

In the spring of 2014, I conducted a qualitative study of 16 campus leaders who held senior-level positions within student affairs. Their positions were represented through a dean of students (3), associate vice president (3), vice president/vice chancellor (9), and senior vice president (1). They were from both public (63%) and private institutions (38%). Participants' background included Indian (6%), African American (13%), and White (81%). Women accounted for 56% of the participants. The number of years of experience was substantial, with 87% of participants having 15 or more years in the field of student affairs and 55% having 20 or more years in the field.

Data included a social media usage survey, individual interviews, and observation of individual Twitter accounts from January through June 2014. After the interviews, 800 of the participants' Twitter posts were analyzed and coded. In this research, tweets, videos, pictures, and blog posts delivered rich data on how senior-level student affairs leaders really use such tools. Survey results revealed that Twitter was the most popular platform used by the participants in their campus leadership role. Comparing 12 available social media platforms, 100% of the participants ranked Twitter as "very important" or "important" to their work professionally. The second most popular platform was Facebook, with 60% rating it "very important" or "important." These results gave weight to observing the participants' Twitter accounts over Facebook for the second part of the study (Ahlquist, 2016).

As a result of this research, I developed two tools to guide student affairs professionals with their digital identity development. This includes a

Figure 2.1. Digital Decision-Making Model

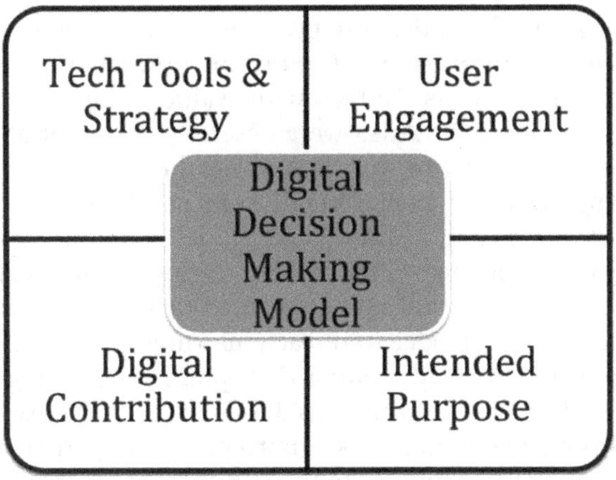

Tech Tools & Strategy	User Engagement
Digital Contribution	Intended Purpose

Digital Decision Making Model

digital decision-making model and a digital leadership framework that challenge professional identity to be blended into a personal yet strategic digital presence.

A Digital Decision-Making Model.   If professionals self-identify in the foundational outcome of the technology competency, they may be asking questions such as: What platform(s) should I be on? What and when do I share? What are my boundaries? Who do I want in my network? What is the value of being on the platform? These are all very common questions, and they will occur every time a new social media platform is released. The answers to these questions are quite unique to each student affairs professional, and they are based upon personal choice. Student affairs professionals can decide intentionally or by trial and error how they make decisions about social media.

To aid in the reflective process, I produced a digital decision-making model that features the methods and rationale that the 16 senior student affairs officers (SSAOs) utilized to incorporate social media into both their professional and personal lives successfully. This model is an especially helpful tool for professionals exploring their digital identity or educating others on digital identity.

Taking a four-pronged social media approach, the digital decision-making model is a representation of the experiences participants shared on social media. The four prongs include connecting tools and skills (digital tools and strategy), intentionally engaging with individuals online (user engagement), selecting content to post (digital contribution), and the reasons why the participants choose their digital activity (intended purpose). A visual of the model is represented in Figure 2.1; it illustrates for student affairs professionals, faculty, and graduate students how digital activity can be strategic, personal, and meaningful. The model is fluid and flexible enough to guide one through a reflective digital identity exercise for social media use.

Technology Tools and Strategy.   This area answers the following questions: What platforms should I be on, and how will I use each tool? As revealed by the participants, 100% saw the value of Twitter, and Facebook (60%) and Instagram (35%) also were described as important. Of special note is that a learning curve was present for the participants, even when learning through trial and error. Overall, student affairs leaders engaged in social media at various points throughout the day; as one associate vice president in the South explained, "I try not to go hog wild, but I will post during the day." In the survey, it was also discovered that the most popular times to participate in social media were early morning (5–7 a.m.), lunchtime (11 a.m.–1 p.m.), and early evening (7–9 p.m.). The average time spent weekly on social media platforms was 3.3 hours, with the participants' usage ranging from 1 to 6 hours weekly. Further, 69% of participants received no support from staff or students to manage their social media accounts.

The following questions should be asked by anyone completing his or her own student affairs digital decision-making model:

1. What social tools are you currently drawn to, and which ones do you have questions and concerns about?
2. Knowing what social media applications your students are on the most, which platforms make sense for your presence as a student affairs professional?
3. What human resources do you have on your campus, especially students, graduate students, and new professionals, who could be your digital mentors, guiding your adoption and exploration of tools?
4. Can you imagine yourself logging on in the early morning, at lunchtime, or in the evening to engage with your campus community?

User Engagement.   This area covers engagement with various digital platforms, especially boundaries set with students and supervisees. Overwhelmingly, the participants expressed comfort in connecting with students on Twitter. A dean of students in the Midwest shared, "I use Twitter really as another tool to engage our students. You know, we've got 16,000 students on campus. So, my office needs to engage and meet all of them." The participants' strategies for connecting with colleagues on campus were similar, as they openly engaged with other student affairs professionals most frequently on Twitter. A vice president in the Southwest explained, "It's [social media] a different way of helping me understand my profession. Both in a sense of on my campus but also national connection to other colleges." Through Twitter, participants were able to connect with the broadest audience.

The approach to Facebook user engagement varied among the participants. Some professionals chose to keep Facebook personal and not accept friend requests from students. One dean of students had a philosophy on "friend-ing" students, stating, "I won't friend a student unless they make a request with me. There are certain privacy settings that I, of course, set on Facebook." Therefore, no matter the platform, the participants had a plan and settings in place for student engagement.

A professional crafting his or her own digital decision-making model would need to consider the makeup of the user engagement prong by asking the following questions:

1. Who are the main audiences with whom you want to engage in your position and in your profession?
2. What is your current comfort level when engaging with students on social media? What about your colleagues, supervisees, national, or international contacts?
3. What resources do you have globally for connecting with other professionals, and how have you balanced connecting with current college students on social media?
4. Who will you connect with, or not connect with, on each social platform? What are the benefits for connecting with those you do allow into your network?

Digital Contribution.   This area is defined as the actual digital content you want to post. Participants made a number of common types of posts, including appreciating others, promoting or posting about events, celebrating holidays, sharing news or information, and responding to others directly. Participants consistently posted and shared tweets that celebrated others, with one vice chancellor explaining, "One of the things I do on Twitter is what I call campus celebrations. So, those are messages that have to do with how my teams are doing, how proud I am of my students, or how proud I am of something the staff has done." In addition, the ability to be positive and constantly conscious of their position was represented in the participant's posts. This included sharing their experiences at campus events, like a basketball game, and getting out real-time information, such as weather advisories.

Part of crafting a student affairs digital decision-making model is deciding what you want to contribute through your social media activity. This can be explored by answering the following questions:

1. Think about the value you hope to contribute to your campus and profession. How does this live out digitally?
2. Are there certain topics, experiences, and/or people you will not post about?

3. What is your comfort level in posting about your campus? Is this supported strategically in offices such as university relations?
4. How can you incorporate your personality and personal life into your social media presence?

Intended Purpose. The study discovered that the senior student affairs leaders hoped for social media to be a significant meaning-making tool beyond marketing. Signing up for Twitter or Periscope just because someone in your division tells you to is not this type of intended purpose. The student affairs leaders shared examples, such as celebrating and lifting up others, making themselves accessible to students, and having a strong sense of the campus by listening on social media. A dean of students in the Midwest stressed,

> I think the first thing is the accessibility piece. I want to be a dean of students that students know my name. I want people to be like, oh, I know (participant name). And I think it's really hard if you're on the campus of 25,000 people. Social media is a value add because you can truly have that presence; you can be the people's dean.

Participants described social media as a tool, especially for instant engagement and real-time information. This is an example of how a vice president approached social media: "The goal is [with technology] to make the connection. And then we can figure out how to move beyond the 140 characters, make it useful. That's really what it is. It's a tool."

These are a few ways in which the student affairs participants applied a deeply intended purpose to their digital identity. The following questions could be asked to complete the student affairs digital decision-making model around intended purpose:

1. What are the values that draw you to the work you do? Are these values present in your approach to social media and your digital identity?
2. What is an outcome you are currently intentionally working on in your position?
3. Have you identified student affairs role models you can look to who are demonstrating intentionality on tools like Twitter, Facebook, or Instagram?
4. How does intentionality currently factor into your digital identity? On which platform can you apply a deeper purpose?

Using this model as a guide to social media adoption, exploration, and experimentation leads student affairs professionals through a discernment process. How does X tool fit into your purpose, enable you to make a contribution, and engage with the right users through the right platform? The model can be used to develop your digital activity as a whole or on a case-by-case basis as new applications arise. The four prongs also provide structure when teaching about digital identity to current and future professionals. This model proposes a blended approach to a genuine digital identity and elevates the value of social media with the campus community, including students.

Digital Identity and Leadership: A Blended Approach to Social Technologies.   As the tech competency calls for ability at the advanced level, professionals must strive not only to develop a genuine digital identity, but also to gain skills at digital leadership in student affairs. With the use of research findings from the SSAOs, I developed a framework for digital practice that blends professional social media use with a personal approach. The digital decision-making model does provide structure, but the proposed Digital Leadership Framework in Student Affairs is a tool more for intermediate and advanced professionals looking to gain and enact digital leadership skills. The four elements that make up the entire Digital Leadership Framework include prioritizing relationships, strategic communications, leadership philosophy, and embracing change. This section will focus on building a genuine and blended digital identity, with the use of the leadership philosophy component of the framework.

The participants demonstrated a number of themes that related to their overall leadership philosophy as a leader in the field. These themes were tied to significant shared values that carried over from in person to online. Three shared philosophies were featured, including being of service to students, fostering a community of care, and embracing a whole-life approach to leadership.

Service to Students.   As this research uncovered, service to students can also be accomplished through social media. The participants expressed a desire not only to connect and communicate with students through social media and face to face, but also to be of service to them, as was shared by a dean of students in the Northeast:

> I think my role is really more to support the students' experience here at [university name]. And in that regard, I want them to feel proud of [institution name]. I want them to celebrate. I want them to learn from, reflect, and recognize all of the things that these students are doing. And so my Twitter connections to students are trying to help them solve their problems or connect them to other people, so that they are aware of the campus resources.

When exploring this philosophy, service to students, the following questions should be answered:

1. How does this philosophy remind you of your own, with or without technology?
2. What are your concerns about interacting with your students on social media?

3. What is one account you would feel the most comfortable experimenting with for this challenge?

Community of Care.   Another major value in the field of student affairs the participants shared was creating a safe and caring community. The results of this research display how this philosophy can live out online. As one vice chancellor stated, "It [social media] lets them [students] know that the institution is really concerned about them. A lot of this, for me, is very about giving people an opportunity to feel validated, just to be who they are." Another participant made use of the immediacy of technology by using Twitter to share information about a campus emergency in real time and to advertise available resources following the tragedy. "Today I saw a counselor to help me cope with the three tragic deaths of #___ [university name] students. Let's work together to end #college #mentalhealth #stigma." The ability of this senior leader to share so openly was connected to a leadership philosophy of community of care, and displayed whole-life leadership as well. When exploring this philosophy, community of care, the following questions should be answered:

1. How does this philosophy remind you of your own, with or without technology?
2. What are your concerns about showing care and concern on social media?
3. What is one account you would feel the most comfortable experimenting with for this social media philosophy?

Whole-Life Leadership.   As campus leaders, the participants took on a philosophy both online and on campus described as "what you see is what you get," meaning who the participants are as leaders on campus is who they are at home. This philosophy was also carried over into their social media activity. A senior vice president in the South stated her whole-life leadership approach, "I think for me it's very comfortable to just try to be as candid and real as possible." Over time, the participants found a comfort level with their digital identity online, sometimes by experimenting on digital platforms. This included bringing out their personality, which was observed in their Twitter posts, which were playful in nature. Participants used Twitter not only to share news, but also pop culture, fitness, and information about their family, children, and pets. For example, a dean of students from the Northeast tweeted, "Just watched @Disney's #Frozen with my niece. My two take-aways: 1. Everyone's a bit of a fixer upper. 2. Some people are worth melting for."

Many tweets from participants also had photos of their families. A senior vice president from the Midwest described the value of sharing personal content,

In a role like mine, personal and professional lives intertwine. My son and wife attend campus events, and wear university gear when we travel. Allowing that intersection to be matched online allows me to be open in my personal interactions and create an authenticity while keeping those interactions sufficiently professional.

When exploring this philosophy, whole-life leadership, the following questions should be answered:

1. How does this philosophy remind you of your own, with or without technology?
2. What are your concerns about sharing your personal life on social media with the campus community?
3. What is one account you would feel the most comfortable experimenting with a blend of both personal and professional content?

The results of this study shed light on how student affairs professionals can approach digital identity with strategic actions and reflection. Social media use as a student affairs professional has many gray areas, such as what applications to be active on and what connections to accept. The blended approach takes into consideration values of social media use, and as a result, contributes to the end product: your student affairs digital identity and leadership potential using technology tools. Lewis and Rush (2013) explained that a digital leader is aware of and able to use technology, is open to experimenting with it, and explores how to incorporate it into the larger community. In the field of K–12 education, Sheninger (2014) proposed that, "Digital leadership focuses on a consistent pursuit of innovation, effective integration of technology, quality of professional development, transparency, celebration of success from which others may learn, establishment of relationships with stakeholders, an open mind, and anticipation of continued change" (p. 23). Taking these definitions one step further for higher education, this research exemplified a blended digital identity and leadership approach that is strategic, yet values based, to interact with the entire campus community, including students (Ahlquist, 2016). Digital leadership in higher education is the "heartware" of tech, connecting software and hardware innovations to relationships and community building.

Though how your digital identity is constructed is currently a personal choice in student affairs, those embracing their digital reputations and committing to digital leadership in the field are making a significant impact. Without digital education to explore digital identity and leadership further, there will continue to be professionals who refuse to join platforms because of false perceptions or make ill-informed digital decisions like creating two Facebook accounts, one for students and one for their "real life." Even worse, they will use tools inappropriately, without recognition that their actions represent their campus. This research exemplified a blended digital identity and leadership approach, whether using a face-to-face or digital platform. The development of a student affairs professional digital identity needs to be seen as a holistic process and an ongoing task, in which adapting to technology is allowed and exploration comes out in personal learning networks. These networks will be the conduit that fuels a student affairs digital identity.

Going #SApro with Personal Learning Networks.   This final approach to a blended digital identity is especially written for educators who are looking to build foundational technology skills in student affairs; however, every student affairs professional needs to work on digital identity, no matter their title, years of experience, or number of Twitter followers. A strategic effort to build digital identity, especially in student affairs, can be made through personal learning networks (PLN), which provide a social network, including one on social media (Siemens, 2005). In a PLN, the user is central to creating his or her network and responsible for contributing and sharing (Guidry & Ahlquist, 2016). With emerging technologies, such as social media, a PLN can be quickly expanded and enhanced.

The tech competency challenges professionals to curate a PLN at each of its levels. At the foundation level, a student affairs professional (#SApro) should, "Engage in personal and professional digital learning communities and personal learning networks at the local, national, and/or global level" (ACPA & NASPA, 2015, p. 33). A primary example of a PLN in student affairs is Twitter. With the use of a hashtag, one can follow organized weekly chats like #sachat, #sagrad, or #emchat; association conference events like #NASPA17 or #ACPA17; or more general content with #sapro, #highered, and #studentaffairs. Barr et al. (2014) also recognized "tweet ups" as connecting a digital tool like Twitter connections with face-to-face gatherings. Professionals should also follow other colleagues at all levels of the field to observe and learn how each professional incorporates different tools into their digital identity.

In addition, there are collaborative PLNs using blogging, YouTube, and podcast platforms to build community and share knowledge. Two examples of these student affairs communities include the Student Affairs Collective and Higher Ed Live. Guidry and Ahlquist (2016) describe these PLNs as follows: "Collaborative spirit is fostered as these projects grow and take on additional contributors" (p. 606). The shift from the foundational to the intermediate level of the tech competency is building PLNs, and contributing to and advancing PLNs occurs at the intermediate and advanced levels.

Personal learning networks introduce student affairs professionals to colleagues, conversations, and resources around the globe 24/7, and they can be used to further expand and explore digital identity. Members of these professional networks can serve as digital role models and digital mentors, as the field continually adapts to evolving technologies. There are various other tools that offer PLNs, including Facebook and LinkedIn groups. However, Barr et al. (2014) warned about the junkyard of the next-big-things in tech, suggesting, "The goal and the focus should be framed in terms of the desired outcomes and not the specific intended vehicle of delivery" (p. 90). In other words, chasing the latest social media tools is a bad strategy. A better tactic is to incorporate tools that fit goals that have been identified and explored through the digital decision-making model.

Conclusion

The aim of this chapter was to challenge perceptions about social technologies, especially in response to the recently revised ACPA and NASPA Professional Competency Areas for Student Affairs Educators. The technology competency asks professionals to be active and consistent contributors on campus and online. At no other time have students and all of society been forced to figure out new digital tools at such a rapid rate—ones with viral capabilities—while progressing down their own developmental paths. Mamta Accapadi, Vice President of Student Affairs at Rollins College reflects,

> Everything that we contribute now is in a space where it becomes our story. How do we educate and prepare our students to the fact that—because of the pieces that they leave behind—people can write their version of your story. (Personal communication, June 2014)

This also holds true for higher education professionals. There are limited resources available to guide one on how to interact on social media with students, staff, and colleagues; however, the results of research on SSAOs provides guidance on how all student affairs professionals can make meaning, take action and demonstrate leadership on social media. The study documented that professionals can make strategic decisions while using social tools through a blended approach, and they are even able to provide value for students in the digital space. These professionals establish how a blended digital identity can also inspire digital leadership in the field of student affairs.

Digital identity education does not fall only on graduate preparation programs or at professional association conferences. Local action and conversations need to be infused at the institutional, divisional, departmental, and individual level. This chapter does not advocate adoption of the latest application or iPhone device; rather, it encourages the consideration of digital actions and the reasons behind them, as well as tools that can take digital identity to a level that will make an impact. Tools such as a decision-making model and a blended approach to digital identity can expand a foundational skill of digital identity into advanced levels of the technology professional competency in student affairs for digital leadership. This type of digital identity can be personal and professional, genuine and purposeful, and an authentic and honest approach to social tools, both when engaging with colleagues in the field of student affairs and educating students about their use.

References

Ahlquist, J. (2015). *Developing digital student leaders: A mixed methods study of student leadership, identity and decision making on social media* (Doctoral dissertation). Retrieved from ProQuest Dissertations and Theses. (Accession No. 3713711).

Ahlquist, J. (2016). Digitally connected: Exploring the social media utilization of senior-level student affairs administrators. Manuscript submitted for publication.

Barr, J. M., McClellen, G. S., & Sandeen, A. (2014). *Making change happen in student affairs.* San Francisco, CA: Jossey-Bass.

boyd, d. (2014). *It's complicated: The social lives of networked teens.* New Haven, CT: Yale University Press.

Cabellon, E.T. (2011, August 29). Digital identity development in higher education [Web log message]. Retrieved from http://edcabellon.com/digitalidentity

Cabellon, E. T. (2016). *Redefining student affairs through digital technology: A ten-year historiography of digital technology use by student affairs administrators* (Doctoral dissertation). Retrieved from ProQuest Dissertations and Theses. (Accession No. 10013238).

Cabellon, E. T., & Junco, R. (2015). The digital age of student affairs. *New Directions for Student Services, 151,* 49–61.

College Student Educators International (ACPA) & Student Affairs Professionals in Higher Education (NASPA). (2015). Professional competency areas for student affairs educators. Retrieved from http://www.naspa.org/images/uploads/main/ACPA_NASPA_Professional_Competencies_FINAL.pdf

Guidry, K., & Ahlquist, J. (2016). Computer-mediated communication and social media. In G. S.McClellan & J. Stringer (Eds.), *The handbook of student affairs administration* (4th ed.). San Francisco, CA: Jossey-Bass.

Junco, R. (2014). *Engaging students through social media: Evidence-based practices for use in student affairs.* San Francisco, CA: Jossey-Bass.

Keller, L. (Producer). (2004). To catch a predator [Television series]. New York, NY: NBC Studios.

Lewis, B., & Rush, D. (2013). Experience of developing Twitter-based communities of practice in higher education. *Research in Learning Technology, 21,* 1–35.

Mahler, J. (2015, March 8). Who spewed that abuse? Anonymous Yik Yak isn't telling. *New York Times.* Retrieved from http://www.nytimes.com/2015/03/09/technology/popular-yik-yak-app-confers-anonymity-and-delivers-abuse.html

Metzler, D., & Smerling, M. (Producers). (2012). Catfish [Television series]. New York, NY: MTV Studios.

Sheninger, E. (2014). *Digital leadership: Changing paradigms for changing times.* Thousand Oaks, CA: Corwin A Sage Company.

Siemens, G. (2005, April 5). Connectivism: a learning theory for the digital age [Web log]. Retrieved from http://www.elearnspace.org/Articles/connectivism.htm

Stoller, E. (2012, September 12). Digital identity development [Web log post]. Retrieved from   http://www.insidehighered.com/blogs/student-affairs-and-technology/digital-identity-development

JOSIE AHLQUIST *is adjunct faculty at Florida State University, Undergraduate Certificate in Leadership Studies program and international digital leadership educator.*

NEW DIRECTIONS FOR STUDENT SERVICES • DOI: 10.1002/ss

3

This chapter describes the opportunity for senior student affairs officers (Ssaos) to develop an increased digital fluency to meet the needs of various constituencies in the digital age. The authors explore what a digital fluency is, how it might impact Ssaos' leadership potential, and the benefits for their respective divisions.

A Strategic Necessity: Building Senior Leadership's Fluency in Digital Technology

Kara Kolomitz, Edmund T. Cabellon

Senior student affairs officers (SSAOs) face evolving innovation opportunities through the successes and challenges brought on by digital and social technologies. Today, the academy's leadership, at all levels of an institution, struggles with allocating the proper resources toward activating technology's potential, from staff time to complementary software and hardware; however, SSAOs also focus on utilizing various digital technologies to engage students throughout their entire life cycle (Cabellon, 2016). Yet, the landscape of higher education continues to shift through the disaggregation of services and pressure to establish new cost models and provide evidence of return on investment (Bowen, 2013; Selingo, 2013).

In the wake of the technological revolution, senior student affairs leadership, provosts, vice presidents, deans of students, and other key senior divisional leaders, have an unprecedented opportunity to develop a technological fluency, imparting to their constituents the essential, critical, and exciting possibilities of digital and social communication. Literature highlights a relationship between the increased use and prevalence of social and digital technologies and increased opportunities for student learning (Junco, 2014). However, senior student affairs leaders hold prominent roles in highlighting and embracing the relevance and influence of digital technology in the lives of the contemporary college student, and the ways in which it resonates and defines a student's identity and support network (Ellison, Steinfield, & Lampe, 2007).

This chapter presents, from the practicalities to the research, the digital mindset and fluency vital to higher education executive leadership, proven implementation practices from senior student affairs leadership,

New Directions for Student Services, no. 155, Autumn 2016 © 2016 Wiley Periodicals, Inc.
Published online in Wiley Online Library (wileyonlinelibrary.com) • DOI: 10.1002/ss.20182

47

strategic implications and benefits for leading digital and social communication efforts on campus, and the potential this role holds in solidifying student affairs as central to an institution. As the higher education landscape continues to evolve, it will be essential for students to be exposed to opportunities, services, and a campus climate directed by confident, germane, and technologically competent student affairs leaders.

A Senior Student Affairs Officer's Digital Mindset

Cabellon and Junco (2015) posited that the digital age calls for practitioners to be technologically fluent, highlighted by a digital mindset to engage students and the growing number of millennial staff members joining student affairs divisions. Although many senior leaders recognize the value of these various digital technologies (Ahlquist, 2016), their use and application vary across all institutions. This has caused dissonance at a time when SSAOs must lead with a purposeful, divisional plan to harness the power and scope of digital and social technologies (Cabellon & Pina, 2016). Literature also indicates social technologies are an integral aspect in the majority of our students' lives (Junco, 2014). Given these emerging bodies of research, a senior leader risks professional competency without an understanding of the digital evolution, its presence, and its future (College Student Educators International [ACPA] & Student Affairs Professionals in Higher Education [NASPA], 2015).

Pearson and Young (2002, p. 11) defined technology literacy as "an understanding of the nature and history of technology, a basic hands-on capability related to technology, and an ability to think critically about technological development." In addition, technologically literate leaders would possess specific knowledge, ways of thinking and acting, and capabilities that assist them as they interact with the technology found in their environments.

Knowledge.

- Recognizes the pervasiveness of technology in everyday life.
- Knows some of the ways technology shapes human history and how people shape technology.
- Knows that all technologies entail risk, some that can be anticipated and some that cannot.
- Acknowledges that the development and use of technology may involve trade-offs and a balance of costs and benefits.
- Understands that contemporary technology reflects the values and culture of the current society.

NEW DIRECTIONS FOR STUDENT SERVICES • DOI: 10.1002/ss

Ways of Thinking and Acting.

- Asks pertinent questions, of self and others, regarding the benefits and risks of various technologies.
- Independently seeks information about new technologies.
- Participates and is engaged in decisions about the development and use of technology.

Capabilities.

- Can demonstrate and articulate a range of hands-on technological skills.
- Could search solutions to technological challenges and roadblocks.
- Can apply basic mathematical concepts related to probability, scale, and estimation to make informed judgments about technological risks and benefits (Pearson & Young, 2002, p. 17)

Although student affairs professionals continue to grow their technology literacy at varying rates, it is the responsibility of SSAOs to discover ways to become fluent, rather than simply literate. White (2013) argued that digital fluency encompasses "the demonstration of various technology skills and knowledge in appropriate administrative and teaching ways" (p. 9). Although administrators may utilize a variety of technological tools for communication, efficiency, or organizational change purposes (Cabellon, 2016), it is the role of the SSAO to provide the leadership, support, resources, and space necessary to showcase and celebrate the effectiveness of digital and social technologies.

The challenge for SSAOs is that a consistent gap exists between literacy and fluency in student affairs. This gap is highlighted by student affairs graduate preparatory programs lacking formal digital technology education throughout its curriculum (Dickerson et al., 2011), to the only recent addition of the student affairs technology competency (ACPA & NASPA, 2015; Herdlein, Riefler, & Mrowka, 2013). Also, digital technology innovations are often implemented at the department level, where professionals have the necessary knowledge and skills, along with the latitude to experiment and discover. To bridge this gap, a reshaping of current staff and budget throughout the entire division would provide the infrastructure to support a hybrid approach to technological support (Stoller, 2014), leading to more intentionality in digital and social technology use division-wide. Having a high level of digital fluency with a wider range of campus technologies may provide more success in serving students and highlight not only the value of the student affairs division, but may also lead to the division becoming a central resource to making meaning of the cocurricular experience in a unique way.

As the annual Beloit College Mindset list presents college student's cultural touchstones and experiences that may have shaped their experiences

New Directions for Student Services • DOI: 10.1002/ss

(Beloit College, 2015), it would behoove SSAOs to recognize their own digital technology mindsets and biases, how they personally and professionally role model digital technology tools, and the priority they give to professional development opportunities. SSAOs might consider the following questions:

- How do you and your division leaders view, understand, and support digital technology implementation?
- How have you role modeled applicable use of digital technology and social communication tools over the last 6 months?
- How have you provided professional development for digital technology and social communication tools for your division over the last 6 months? Additionally, how have you recognized and rewarded those who have been innovative in their use of these tools?

Supported by Ahlquist's research presented in the previous chapter, these fundamental questions provide a foundation for SSAOs to provide a holistically integrated approach to digital technology inclusion throughout the division, rather than only at the department level. Additionally, the expectations for the implementation of digital technologies are made evident for divisional directors through this intentional leadership.

One way SSAOs might actualize their digital mindset would be through the reallocation of budgetary and human resources. Kuk (2012) noted that the changing nature of student affairs are forcing senior leadership to rethink previous spending and staffing structures to support their programs and services reaching a wider audience. For example, instead of department heads being given a budget toward printing flyers, posters, and programs, these funds might be redistributed for paid social media ads or the use of mobile applications, such as Guidebook, to replace paper copies. Student affairs administrators gain the ability to also analyze digital data, which Liz Gross and Jason Meriwether cover in their chapter within this volume.

Certainly, the larger the institution, the greater the flexibility SSAOs have to create new roles throughout the division to actualize their digital mindset. Tull and Kuk (2012) highlight the depth and variety of these new roles, including Directors of Marketing and Communication or Technology, Assistant to the Vice President, or Chief of Staff. These roles vary in scope and organizational position, but are becoming more common as the need for leadership in digital areas become more important. Overall, as SSAOs develop and embrace a digital mindset, their ability to actualize it deeply depends on their resource and talent management skills.

Senior Student Affairs Officers' Leadership in the Digital Age

The complexity caused by the academy's evolution calls leaders to bring about their digital fluency in meaningful ways (Barr, McClellan, & Sandeen,

2014). There are three reasons why senior student affairs officers should actively engage in digital technologies and support their use more fully. First, the creation, support and implementation of a technology competency provides the necessary framework for SSAOs to develop the best ways their divisions can lead their respective institutions. This framework is guided by two overarching themes: that technology application should be focused on the holistic, developmental work of student affairs educators and that innovation should drive its use, highlighting its dynamic nature in engaging students throughout the learning process. The 2015 College Student Educators International–ACPA Presidential Task Force on Digital Technology report identified the responsibility for the sustainability and importance of technology resting with student affairs leadership. Cabellon and Doody (2015) noted, "This includes a movement towards dedicated staff division and cabinet leadership who have a strong fluency in digital technology in a higher education environment, with the ability to educate, guide, and inspire others" (paragraph 16).

Second, contemporary leadership in higher education requires a deeper understanding and application of digital technology to connect properly and engage with a wider constituency base from prospective and current students to alumni and community members (Whitt & Schuh, 2015). For example, a number of university presidents are successfully role modeling leadership through their digital communication efforts (Garner, 2015). President Santa Ono at the University of Cincinnati is often referred to as a role model, boasting more than 41,000 followers on Twitter, and utilizing his platform to engage the university's members and beyond. In addition, Nolan (2013) asserted that in higher education, social media is everyone's job, particularly those in leadership. He referenced the importance of enrollment services, particularly recruitment: "If you are not active on social media, you are not contributing to the recruitment of the incoming class. You are probably not [sic] really doing your job, as I (and a growing number of others) see it" (Nolan, 2013, paragraph 12).

Third, active and intentional leadership in digital technology provides practitioner evidence of its usefulness and effectiveness. For example, in 2011, 2012, and 2013, Kenn Elmore, the dean of students at Boston University (BU) created videos to promote the annual BU Class Gift campaign. By partnering with the Development and Video Production studios on campus, his creative videos enticed seniors to participate in the annual campaign through a promise to jump into the Charles River in Boston, MA if the campaign goals were met. These videos utilized Mr. Elmore's creativity, personality, and application of YouTube to achieve their perspective goals each year. Although some senior staff members may not go to these extremes to hit fundraising goals, the utilization of YouTube along with other social networks to amplify and share the goals related to these campaigns served as a community-building platform throughout the academic year for other important messages delivered from the Dean of Students' office.

Additionally, in 2014, Dr. Jason Pina, vice president of student affairs and enrollment management at Bridgewater State University (BSU) supported an initiative to create centralized, student-focused communication platform utilizing a mobile-focused Web site: BSUlife.com. Cabellon (2015) noted that the platform utilized student communication, marketing, and business majors to develop content focused on the student experience. Additionally, these efforts catalyzed the development of an integrated marketing team for the division of student affairs. This team focused on creating a more unified, sophisticated approach to sharing important information and stories for students. By developing an infrastructure of student marketing, graphic design, and communication majors to support this endeavor, the division went from creating single messages to creative campaigns utilizing engaging graphics, short videos, and brief stories to share the story of student life at BSU.

Finally, at smaller institutions, cabinet members, especially the president, are critical to harnessing the leadership power of digital fluency. Dr. Carolyn "Biddy" Martin, president at Amherst College, boasts over 6,000 followers on Twitter, where she regularly engages her community, by actively replying to tweets, re-sharing content, and highlighting their school mascot. Another example is Dr. Ronnie Nettles from Copiah-Lincoln Community College, who genuinely shares a balance of his work and family lives. These examples provide a wide spectrum of opportunities for executives and senior leaders to engage with their respective audiences (Ahlquist, 2014). SSAOs must lead digital technology efforts through building new infrastructure to support its innovative use throughout their respective divisions. Recent academic scholarship combined with administrative practice may further illuminate meaningful integration ideas for institutions of all sizes.

Strategic Benefits for SSAOs and Their Divisions

The shifting and tenuous landscape of higher education calls upon SSAOs to be strategic and forward thinking when leading a student affairs division. A digital mindset is fundamental to contemporary and innovative SSAO leadership, and positions both SSAOs and their division as essential to the institution. Barr et al. (2014, p. 184) suggested student affairs leadership should use this era of the profession to be seen as entrepreneurial change agents on campus: "They understand the value of teamwork and collaboration with their president's, administrative peers, and faculty, but at the same time they recognize that if meaningful change is to occur, it will largely be the result of their own skill."

This key positioning situates student affairs as integral to the presidential cabinet and assures decision-making opportunities, greater visibility institution-wide, and leadership of significant institutional initiatives.

By leveraging a fluency in digital technologies, a senior student affairs leader can use digital data to provide evidence that their services and cocurricular opportunities connect with students. These data, such as Website traffic or social network statistics, can be used to inform student affairs professionals how to connect with a traditional on-campus student population, online students, parents, prospective students, and alumni worldwide. Conversely, digital data also help to inform and guide divisional practice, provide real-time assessment of services and learning outcomes, and influence staffing and resources (Manning, Kinzie, & Schuh, 2013). In a climate of higher education that faces major challenges to securing and increasing resources on campuses, the use of these data can be both affirming and influential in decision-making and resource allocation.

Although senior student affairs officers may have the ability to lead their colleagues and the presidential cabinet in digital and social technology endeavors, the board of trustees should also be considered as key constituents to involve and enlighten. Intentionally communicating, directly or indirectly, the ways in which technologies are being used by a student affairs division should be a priority. Using your leadership, the campaign of a digital mindset is constant, thought provoking, and pervasive; every community member must be considered. As a senior student affairs officer evidences cabinet-level collaboration to the provost, president, and ultimately the board, the digital mindset permeates the institution. The advantages to including a wider constituency in digital fluency efforts may be reflected in the commitment the institution makes to a SSAO's professional development and the opportunities to expand and produce scholarship.

A student affairs division can demonstrate their understanding and support for student learning in every sense through intentional and an interdependent connection with faculty, assuring cocurricular learning, establishing partnerships, and collaborative initiatives. Digital and social technologies can enhance student performance and engagement, inside of and outside of the classroom (Fried, 2008; Junco, 2012). Seamless, cocurricular, and experiential learning opportunities speak to many learning outcomes of student affairs divisions. Consider the ways in which digital citizenship, coupled with student affairs support of furthering student engagement and learning, validate a division's purpose and institutional standing. There are inherent risks and concerns with citizenship and character building in relation to digital and social technologies, and providing intentional learning opportunities for students that address these formative issues is as relevant in contemporary higher education as a student choosing an area of academic study.

The opportunity for student affairs to showcase students' abilities and aptitudes to "lead the learning" on campus is profound, and senior student affairs leaders are uniquely positioned to ensure students' expertise and intelligence is recognized within the context of social and digital technologies. Programs that expose faculty or staff to one-on-one tutoring with a tech-savvy student have begun, and resulted in increased faculty and student participation in the use of emerging technologies (Weaver & Nilson,

2005). The strategy behind being technologically fluent should be a sincere and unwavering commitment to knowing and understanding contemporary students. Student's lives are shaped by these ubiquitous technologies, impacting their personal life and educational process, while raising points of consternation and celebration (Junco, 2014).

These overall benefits might be achieved if SSAOs are strategic in their future approaches. If we are committed to student success and meeting students where they are, senior student affairs leadership must be willing to shift, change, and augment the foundation of their practice to support student's educational and learning efforts fully. Cabellon (2016) offered three ways SSAOs could accomplish this. First, build capacity by redesigning student affairs leadership teams to include a professional with a digital mindset and fluency. These types of professionals can actualize SSAOs' digital technology implementation ideas and plans. If this position cannot be added, then the SSAO must develop a digital mindset and fluency through additional education or by bringing in a consultant to assist.

Next, augment engagement by creating a divisional technology committee to develop technology-related professional development opportunities, and practitioner-based handbooks and guides to assist student affairs administrators in their technology implementation efforts. In addition, this committee may also serve as a divisional technology project review board. When departments request various technological needs (for example, software, hardware), centralize the process through this technology committee.

Third, catalyze change by creating strategic partnerships with colleagues in information technology and institutional communications and marketing, inviting them to assess divisional technology and digital communication efforts. The recommendations from assessment can help prioritize what types of infrastructure a leadership team can invest in to move these efforts from a decentralized to a hybrid model.

In addition, augment engagement by investing in and implementing the use of video throughout the division, including:

1. Add Web cams to older desktops and laptops and provide a video chat option (for example, Skype®, Google Plus®, Hangout, FaceTime®) wherever contact information is posted (Web site, e-mail signature).
2. Record all divisional professional development offerings and post videos publically on YouTube® or through a university-sponsored video hosting service for internal viewing only.
3. Ensure that all divisionally produced videos are captioned for accessibility. Whether the videos tell an important story about the division or are part of enrollment services' admissions or alumni campaigns, this is an important step that must be included in video production.

Finally, catalyze change by having important conversations with student affairs staff about the psychological impact of digital technology, both personally and professionally. For example, encourage staff and students alike to think critically about how they communicate online and how it represents the university. Additionally, create more opportunities for staff and students to disconnect from electronic communication regularly, and model this behavior to present congruent leadership behavior.

Conclusion

A senior leader who has intentionally developed digital fluency is committed to moving higher education and student affairs practice into a new frontier, understands the significance of digital technologies and social media in students' lives, and is strategic in threading these innovations throughout the area of the institution they lead. SSAOs whose leadership stresses the essential, critical, and exciting possibilities of digital and social communication shows responsiveness to new cost structures, new deliverables, student need, and employer need. The landscape of higher education is changing. Significant demographic trends and evolving dimensions of the student population are instigating a new course for the higher education community (Selingo, 2013), one that must address and respond to the rise of the digital age. Therefore, finding tools to engage all students, graduate, undergraduate, online, adult learners, and those on virtual or satellite campuses, is an inevitable need and challenge for student affairs divisions. Further, a digitally fluent SSAO promotes the integration of technologies with teaching and learning in both curricular and cocurricular arenas. Substantial benefits are accrued in recognizing and leading digital and social communication efforts on campus, and these initiatives strategically position student affairs as central to an institution

References

Ahlquist, J. (2014, July 10). Higher education presidents to follow [Web log message]. Retrieved from http://www.josieahlquist.com/2014/07/10/twitterpresidents/2/

Ahlquist, J. (2016). *Digitally connected: Exploring the social media utilization of senior-level student affairs administrators*. Manuscript submitted for publication.

Barr, M. J., McClellan, G. S., & Sandeen, A. (2014). *Making change happen in student affairs*. San Francisco, CA: Jossey-Bass.

Beloit College. (2015). The mindset list for the class of 2015. Retrieved from https://www.beloit.edu/mindset/previouslists/2015/

Bowen, W. G. (2013). *Higher education in the digital age*. Princeton, NJ: Princeton University Press.

Cabellon, E. (2015). A student affairs integrated communication strategy (Web log). Retrieved from http://edcabellon.com/interests/studentaffairscommunicationstrategy/

Cabellon, E. T. (2016). *Redefining student affairs through digital technology: A ten-year historiography of digital technology use by student affairs administrators* (Doctoral dissertation). Retrieved from ProQuest Dissertations and Theses. (Accession No. 10013238).

Cabellon, E., & Doody, T. (2015). ACPA digital task force draft report. Retrieved from http://digitaltaskforce.myacpa.org/draftreportandrecs

Cabellon, E. T., & Junco, R. (2015). The digital age of student affairs. *New Directions for Student Services, 151,* 49–61.

Cabellon, E., & Pina, J. (2016). An integrated student communication strategy: bsulife.com. Retrieved from http://www.naspa.org/publications/leadership-exchange

College Student Educators International (ACPA) & Student Affairs Professionals in Higher Education (NASPA). (2015). Professional competency areas for student affairs educators. Retrieved from http://www.naspa.org/images/uploads/main/ACPA_NASPA_Professional_Competencies_FINAL.pdf

Dickerson, A. M., Hoffman, J. L., Anan, B. P., Brown, K. F., Vong, L. K., Bresciani, M. J., Monzon, R., & Oyler, J. (2011). A comparison of senior student affairs officer and student affairs preparatory program faculty expectations of entry-level professionals' competencies. *Journal of Student Affairs Research and Practice, 48*(4), 463–479.

Ellison, N. B., Steinfield, C., & Lampe, C. (2007). The benefits of Facebook "friends". Social capital and college students' use of online social network sites. *Journal of Computer-Mediated Communication, 12*(4), 1143–1168.

Fried, C. (2008). In-class laptop use and its effects on student learning. *Computers & Education, 50*(3), 906–914.

Garner, L. (2015, January). College presidents get their own guide to social media. *The Chronicle of Higher Education.* Retrieved from http://chronicle.com/article/College-Presidents-Get-Their/151049/

Herdlein, R., Riefler, L., & Mrowka, K. (2013). An integrative literature review of student affairs competencies: A meta-analysis. *Journal of Student Affairs Research and Practice, 50*(3), 250–269.

Junco, R. (2012). The relationship between frequency of Facebook use, participation in Facebook activities, and student engagement. *Computers & Education, 58*(1), 162–171.

Junco, R. (2014). *Engaging students through social media: Evidence based practices for use in student affairs.* San Francisco, CA: Jossey-Bass.

Kuk, L. (2012). The changing nature of student affairs. In A. Tull & L. Kuk (Eds.), *New realities in the management of student affairs* (pp. 3–12). Sterling, VA: Stylus.

Manning, K., Kinzie, J., & Schuh, J. H. (2013). *One size does not fit all: Traditional and innovative models of student affairs practice.* New York, NY: Routledge.

Nolan, J. M. (2013, September). In higher education, social media is your job. *The Huffington Post.* Retrieved from http://www.huffingtonpost.com/dr-james-michael-nolan/in-higher-education-socia_b_3932373.html

Pearson, G., & Young, A. T. (2002). *Technically speaking: Why all Americans need to know more about technology.* Washington, DC: National Academies Press.

Selingo, J. J. (2013). *College unbound: The future of higher education and what it means for students.* New York, NY: Houghton Mifflin.

Stoller, E. (2014). 5 ways to grow your digital fluency. *Inside Higher Ed.* Retrieved from https://www.insidehighered.com/blogs/student-affairs-and-technoleogy/5-ways-grow-your-digital-fluency

Tull, A., & Kuk, L. (Eds.). (2012). *New realities in the management of student affairs.* Sterling, VA: Stylus.

Weaver, B. E., & Nilson, L. B. (2005). Laptops in class: What are they good for? What can you do with them? *New Directions for Teaching and Learning, 101,* 3–13.

White, G. K. (2013). Digital fluency: Skills necessary for learning in the digital age. Australian Council for Educational Research. Retrieved from http://research.acer.edu.au/cgi/viewcontent.cgi?article=1006&context=digital_learning

Whitt, E. J., & Schuh, J. H. (2015). Glancing back at *New Directions for Student Services*. *New Directions for Student Services*, *151*, 1997–2014.

KARA KOLOMITZ *is vice president for student affairs and enrollment at Regis College.*

EDMUND T. CABELLON *is assistant to the vice president of student affairs and enrollment management at Bridgewater State University and the former co-chair of ACPA's Presidential Task Force on Digital Technology.*

This chapter explores how digital and social technologies may be impacting the developmental journeys of traditionally aged college students. It provides important conceptual distinctions and explores the application of college student development theory in digital spaces along with implications for practice and inquiry.

College Student Development in Digital Spaces

Paul Gordon Brown

Introduction

Contemporary college students in the United States are learning and developing during a unique time—a time period during which social media, digital technologies, and the Internet are ever present. Traditionally aged college students (18–22) are of particular interest as they represent the first generation to have grown up alongside these technologies (Prensky, 2001). The World Wide Web has existed their entire lives, and social media was omnipresent during their teenage years. The smartphone and other forms of mobile technology have also changed teenagers' relationships with social media (Boyd, 2014). These devices made social media and the Web more affordable and nearly ubiquitous, and rearranged the barriers to access across all demographics (Perrin & Duggan, 2015; Smith, Rainie, & Zickuhr, 2011). Given the unique aspects of social and digital technologies and their ascendance during a crucial period of learning and development for today's traditionally aged college students, it is important that educators review their assumptions and applications of theory in light of these changes. Put simply, college student development theory must be applied differently and reexamined for a new digital age.

This chapter explores the impact of social and digital technologies on college students. First, the label of college students as "digital natives" alongside statistics on college student technology use is reviewed. Next, through a review of literature, important concepts including distinguishing between digital identities, something students must be educated about, and digitized development, which students must be guided through, are highlighted. After making this distinction, the remainder of the chapter focuses on the impact of social and digital technologies on student development. This topic will be explored from the viewpoint of existing theory and

NEW DIRECTIONS FOR STUDENT SERVICES, no. 155, Autumn 2016 © 2016 Wiley Periodicals, Inc.
Published online in Wiley Online Library (wileyonlinelibrary.com) • DOI: 10.1002/ss.20183

interrogate how technology may be fundamentally changing the assumptions upon which these traditional theories are built.

College Student Social and Digital Technology Use

The Web and social media were always present for this current generation of students. Marc Prensky (2001) referred to this generation as "digital natives"—a generation for whom these technologies should be assumed. The danger in the "native" label, however, is that it cannot be assumed that although students might have grown up with technology in their surroundings, they are equally savvy in their use of social and digital technologies or that they had equal access to the technology as they were growing up. Regardless of the problematic nature of the label, it surfaces an important reality—that today's emerging adults were surrounded by social and digital technology as they developed. Even if their access was limited as a result of their socioeconomic status or because of parental rules and restrictions, students have nevertheless felt social media's presence.

Statistics on college student use of the Internet, technological devices, and social media reveal a population that is highly connected and networked. The Pew Internet and American Life Project's 2015 survey found that 96% of adults in America, ages 18–29 years old, use the Internet—a nearly universal figure that is likely even higher for students attending college (Perrin & Duggan, 2015). Access to the Internet is also increasingly occurring on mobile devices. As of 2013, approximately 80% of college students report accessing the Internet through their smartphones (Dahlstrom, Walker, & Dziuban, 2013). When they are on their smartphones, an overwhelming majority of college students use these devices for social media. Approximately 88% of students report engaging in social networks and other social software (Smith et al., 2011). Furthermore, these students are accessing multiple social media sites at multiple points in the day (Junco, 2012; Pempek, Yermolayeva, & Calvert, 2009). As a result, this age group is immersed in social media at a higher rate than any other demographic group.

In order to understand the developmental experiences of these emerging adults, examining the impact of digital and social technologies on their lived experience is essential. These students, who are at a critical time in their own growth and development, look to social media as important sites for learning and self-exploration. Research into understanding the impact of these technologies, however, is still relatively nascent, albeit growing, especially for research into the impact of social media on college student development (Junco, 2014).

Research and Key Concepts

Although qualitative research, in particular, on college students and social media is relatively scarce, there are researchers who have contributed greatly to our understating of social and digital technologies' potential impact. For years, MIT sociologist Turkle researched the relationship between human beings and technology and how technology is influencing human behavior. As noted, Turkle (2004) wanted to explore "not only what the computer [is] doing for us, but what it [is] doing to us [emphasis added]" (paragraph 6). This conceptualization of technology as not just a tool, but as something that actually changes the user and the user's decisions and actions, is important. Contemporary college students, by virtue of growing up alongside technology instead of coming to it later in life, are having a profoundly different experience than those who came before them.

Boyd's (2014) research into teenagers' use of social media places these experiences in a time-based context and provides an important starting point for understanding the precollege life of today's students. In particular, Boyd (2014) identified that the virtual community spaces created by social media can be understood as "networked publics" or the community spaces created by social technologies as well as the communities that arise out of the collective use of these technologies. Online communities, affinity groups, message boards, and friendship networks are all examples of networked publics.

Digital networked publics also carry specific properties that make them unique from their physical world counterparts. These unique properties are the "affordances" of technology—"the capabilities that allow [individuals] to act and interact with each other in novel ways that are difficult or were impossible to do in earlier online or offline settings" (Kane, Alavi, Labianca, & Borgatti, 2014, p. 276). Digital affordances are the new possibilities for being, behavior, and action that the online space allows. One example of a new affordance provided by social media technologies is "spreadability" (Boyd, 2014). Spreadability denotes the ease of sharing content in the digital space. In particular, what sets this affordance apart from sharing information in the physical world is digital information's ability to be shared nearly instantaneously and to multiple individuals, who themselves may be geographically distributed. This affordance of social media was not possible when human action was solely relegated to the physical world.

Social media's networked publics, and the affordances these technologies allow, have changed the landscape of human action, communication, and relationships. Understood through an ecological theory lens (Bronfenbrenner, 1993), the environment for behavior is changed. Additionally, the range of possible behaviors in which college students can engage is also altered. Human behaviors are increasingly mediated and structured by the technological tools they use. For educators, this shift requires an understanding of technology that goes beyond mere use and toward a more fundamental understanding of how a technology works and influences the user.

A number of researchers have begun to explore how these digital affordances and spaces are impacting college students. One of the first studies to approach the topic, specifically as it relates to college students, was conducted by Martinez Alemán and Lynk Wartman (2009). In their study, they probed how college students explored and made meaning of their identities. This work was furthered by recently published dissertations which included an examination of how social media impacts college student leaders and their leadership development (Ahlquist, 2015), how social media alters how college students conceptualize and enact principles of civic engagement (Gismondi, 2015), and how social media impacts college student identity, self-presentation, meaning making, and discourse (Brown, 2016; Eaton, 2015). New research represents promising first steps in understanding the lived experience of college students online and the impact of digital and social technology on college student development.

Digital Identities Versus Digitized Development

Central to understanding the impact of social and digital technologies on the developmental process is an understanding of the distinction between two concepts: digital identities and digitized development. The former term, *digital identities*, refers to the various presentations, personas, and constructions of an individual in the online space. This differs from the latter concept, *digitized development*, which is the psychological process of growth and self-learning that occurs when digital contexts are introduced (Brown, 2016). Both of these concepts are related, often informing one another, but are distinct. In practice, however, these two concepts are often conflated under the term *digital identity development* and confusingly referenced informally in casual discourse.

One of the few, and first, mentions of the term *digital identity* in student affairs academic literature defined digital identity as "the composite of images that individuals present, share, and promote for themselves in the digital domain" (Dalton & Crosby, 2013, p. 1). Digital identity, however, can be understood as far more than just the data of an individual online. A more nuanced understanding recognizes that one can have multiple digital identities and that these identities are not static. Instead, digital identities are coconstructed with others who may be interacting with or consuming the content of these identities (Brown, 2016; Martínez Alemán & Lynk Wartman, 2009). An example of the relativity of digital identities can been seen through a potential outcome of context collapse; that is, what occurs when information posted online is intended for one audience but is consumed and interpreted differently by a different audience (Boyd, 2014). In the case of a college student, a student may post content intended for their peers, but it is viewed by and interpreted very differently by a parent or future employer. Digital identities are thus not solely under the control of the individual from which they arise.

Individuals, however, do have agency in the curation and impression management of their digital identities. Engaging in this process is referred to as *digital reputation management* or *personal branding* (Junco, 2014;

NEW DIRECTIONS FOR STUDENT SERVICES • DOI: 10.1002/ss

Qualman, 2015). Where confusion often arises is when reputation management is referred to as *digital identity development*. In using the term *digital identity development*, it is easy to conflate the psychosocial and cognitive processes behind how these identities are constructed with the curation of images and data. Although the two concepts (presentation and development) are certainly related, how one understands oneself and how one is able (or not able) to influence one's self-presentation online are two distinct concepts. In other words, a student's ability to engage in reputation management may be influenced by his or her developmental level, and actively engaging in this curation may push developmental boundaries, but digital identities themselves are not developmental processes.

Conflating presentation and development is problematic (Junco, 2014); however, teaching students about their digital identities and the rules associated with reputation management remain important educational outcomes for college students (Brown, 2016; Qualman, 2015). Educators can help students at all developmental levels by teaching guidelines about what to post and what not to post when interacting online. For example, a student can be taught a rule that states "do not post pictures on social media of yourself drinking alcohol." This rule will generally serve a student well as an emerging adult.

Education on digital reputation, however, can be taken a step further and reach toward developmental outcomes whereby the student understands how, why, and in what contexts they can make judgments about when to apply a rule. Educators can help students by going beyond the provision of rules and engaging students in critical dialogue about the consequences of online and offline actions and the relationship between the two. This type of developmental intervention aids students in contextualizing and internalizing rules of reputation. This more advanced capability requires students to navigate the complex and overlapping contexts of the digital space and is referred to as *digitized development*.

Digitized development takes into account the totality of student behavior and action in both online and offline contexts. Under digitized development, the environment in which a student learns and grows expands to include a digital social space where the affordances of these technologies allow behaviors and actions that are different than those in the offline-only world. Digitized development recognizes that just because someone might be considered highly developed in an offline context does not necessarily mean that, when confronted with the new online world of social media for the first time, they possess the same level of sophistication.

For example, contrast the experiences of a college student who has been on social media for a number of years with that of a parent who, at middle age, may be logging on to social media for the first time. Although not always the case, it is likely that offline the parent operates at a higher developmental capacity than their student. And yet, when it comes to engaging on social media, the parent needs to navigate an entirely new

New Directions for Student Services • DOI: 10.1002/ss

environment with a new set of rules, norms, and affordances. In this situation, the student may be savvier than their parent. This savviness goes beyond a mere understanding of how the technology works and extends to knowledge about online community norms, behaviors, and relationships. The student, however, being at an earlier stage in their development, may have a more limited capacity than their parent for making sense of the online environment. In some ways, the parent and the student each possess something the other lacks.

Digitized development, however, goes further than just one's development level and one's savviness in navigating the digital spaces. Digitized development includes an understanding of how one's actions and relationships online can influence one's actions and relationships offline, and vice versa. This developmental capacity is likely something that neither the parent nor the student masters to a great extent. Furthermore, given the rapid pace of technological change, the context of the online world can change more quickly than our ability to adapt to it. As technologies provide new affordances, or opportunities for action, they may lead to new behaviors that were not previously seen in the offline world.

Further complicating these concepts is the extent to which individuals allow their lives, and by extension their development, to become digitized. Students may immerse themselves online to various degrees and utilize social and digital tools in various ways. Depending on a student's engagement online, they may lead highly digitized lives or none at all. Students leading highly digitized lives view technology as providing immersive digital social environments, whereas those with less digitized lives may see technology as merely a set of tools to be used (Brown, 2016). As students may be increasingly living digitized lives, the next section explores how foundational theories of student development may need to be applied differently or modified to account for digitization.

Applying Developmental Theory to Digital Spaces

Most contemporary theories of college student development were largely developed prior to social media and advancements in personal technology. These advancements enabled new affordances and precipitated environmental changes that made the college student experience different from those of students in the past. Foundational theories, however, are still useful for understanding student behaviors in these online contexts, but the theories must be applied in new ways. For example, the Chickering and Reisser (1993) classic theory of development outlines seven vectors through which students develop over the course of their time in college. One of these vectors, "moving through autonomy towards interdependence" is readily seen in college student behaviors online. In particular, one of the three components of this vector, emotional independence, is evident as students seek "freedom from continual and pressing needs for reassurance, affection, or approval from others" (Chickering & Reisser, 1993, p. 117). In online spaces, college students working through the vector often exhibit approval-seeking behaviors. For example, one of the ways approval is quantified online is through the "Like" or the "Favorite." "Liking" something is a social media action common to many platforms that indicates engagement with a piece of content. Although its exact meaning is somewhat ambiguous, Facebook (2015, paragraph 1) defines a "Like" as "an easy way to let people know that you enjoy it without leaving a comment."

In my research, participants frequently mentioned that either their own or their peers' behaviors are influenced by a compulsion to accumulate a large number of Likes on their social media posts (Brown, 2016). Likes act as a form of external validation—validation that one has worth, validation that what one is expressing is interesting, or validation that one is "important." Under this line of thinking, the more Likes a post receives, the more positively a user is perceived. Likes, particularly the rapid accrual of Likes, indicates worth, and one's worth is on display for others to see. Seeking a large number of Likes also influences what students choose to post on social media. This often leads to individuals posting only the "happy," "exciting," or "extreme" moments in their lives. Given the connected nature of mobile technologies and social media, this compulsion can reach a frenzied pace and consume a student's thoughts and often distort their sense of self-worth. Given the unique properties and affordances of the online space, the impact of competition and comparison behaviors can be heightened.

The importance of receiving Likes parallels behaviors one would find in the physical world from students seeking external validation and relying on external formulas to define their self-worth. Although these behaviors are consistent with the Chickering and Reisser (1993) vector of moving toward emotional independence, these are also consistent with Baxter Magolda's (1999, 2001) theory of self-authorship. Baxter Magolda (2001) posited that college students move from external definition, by others, toward internal definition, describing what is important for them. As students move through college and toward self-authorship, they begin to question the need for external validation through Likes and begin to establish their own self-concept. In short, college students move from being owned by social media to owning social media (Brown, 2016).

The previous example is one way in which online behavior can be understood within the frameworks of existing theories. Attention-seeking social media posts, the ability (or inability) to manage emotions, engagement in identity play, and many other behaviors are also worthy of further exploration. The point in presenting the previous example is less to provide an exhaustive analysis and instead to introduce the notion that concepts from foundational theories, such as those presented in the above examples from Chickering and Reisser (1993) and Baxter Magolda (1999, 2001), are still useful and applicable in attempting to understand college students online.

NEW DIRECTIONS FOR STUDENT SERVICES • DOI: 10.1002/ss

College student educators already have some of the tools to begin to understand and engage students online. The scenarios in which developmental theories are applied may look different because of the digital context, but the theories are still applicable.

Developing New Theory

The previous section demonstrated how existing theory could be applied to understanding college student behavior online in digital and social media spaces. Although this is a useful approach, the advancement of technology and the increasingly blurry boundaries between and within online and offline contexts causes one to question if the underlying concepts in foundational theories still hold in all instances, including concepts of linearity, stage-based progression, and desirable developmental goals and outcomes. The relationships between a student's online life and identities and their offline life and identities are increasingly complex, a reason Majchrzak (2009, p. 18) encourages practitioners to understand digital and social technologies "in terms of affordances, functionalities, and behavioral use patterns." In other words, the emphasis is on what the technologies allow individuals to do, such as the actions, abilities and potentialities these spaces and tools create. Knowing a specific social media site or tool is therefore less important than understanding the environment it provides and the behavior it enables.

Those who use digital technologies create new environments and new means and opportunities for expression without the baggage of physical world rules and norms because these tools are free from the constraints of the physical world. It is the digital space as a virtual space that creates a unique developmental environment with characteristics and opportunities that differ from the physical world, that enables individuals to "act and interact with each other in novel ways that are difficult or were impossible to do in earlier online or offline settings" (Kane et al., 2014, p. 276). College students, in particular, are well placed to leverage technology and explore these new possibilities for action. These new potentialities also have theoretical implications as they may "undermine or violate the assumptions of established theory, potentially requiring researchers to adapt these theories for application to social media settings or possibly develop new ones" (Kane et al., 2014, p. 276).

Within the college context, the potential for theoretical disruption should cause educators to question if the nature of college student identity and self is changing—a fairly radical notion. Postmodern theorists have been describing this change for decades. They recognize an evolving self that is increasingly "fragmented" (Seider & Gardner, 2009, April), "saturated" (Gergen, 2011), and "fluid" (Côté, 2005) as a result of the intersection of self with technology. In practice, traditionally aged college students, on the forefront of technological change, may be struggling to make sense of this new reality just as much as educators. Given that trends toward increasing integration with technology show no sign of abating, and may even be accelerating, it is increasingly important that college student development theory be revised and/or new theory be constructed. Much like the paradigmatic move in science from Newtonian physics, to theories of relativity and quantum mechanics, constructions of theory in digital spaces may not follow neat, stage-based developmental patterns but instead recognize identity and developmental movement as being more fluid. The construction of narratives, and the idea of performativity and identity correspondence, may also become more salient as avenues for inquiry. A number of queer, critical, and postmodern theorists are already moving in this direction, and there are parallels with what may be occurring in the digital space (Patton, Renn, Guido, & Quaye, 2016). Foundational theories, although still useful, may nevertheless fail to capture increasing complexities of identity and self for today's college students. Although society is far from understanding all of the ramifications of these technologies, educators must figure out how to help students navigate these realities.

Putting Theory Into Practice

When reflecting on the concepts of digital identities versus digitized development, and how college student development in social media and digital spaces may be changing, there are a number of implications for college student educator practice. All of the concepts provide useful guideposts, but practitioners need to apply different lenses to varying degrees as situations warrant and as technology evolves. Because of the rapid pace of technological change, the following recommendations are intended to provide broad advice likely to hold up over time.

Partnering With Students can Help Increase One's Own Understanding of Digital and Social Technology and Help Students in Their Navigation of it.   As a result of the explosion in social media, traditionally aged college students are receiving messages from more contexts than ever before. In particular, students are experiencing a confusing time of upheaval as norms are disrupted and new norms need to be established. With increased access to information and messages being consumed, students may have difficulty managing and making sense of these messages (Kegan, 1994). Rather than having a small group of mentors and educators providing guidance, students may experience multiple competing messages from multiple sources, without the tools or developmental capacity to make choices and commitments (Seider & Gardner, 2009, April). Furthermore, as a result of a delayed or prolonged period of emerging adulthood, contemporary college students are having difficulty developing purpose and making meaning of their lives (Arnett, 2005). Participation in social media may represent a double-edged sword for a student. On the one hand it allows for new avenues of exploration and expression; on the other it exponentially increases the amount of information one is exposed to and the number of choices one must make.

To aid students in navigating an explosion of information and choices, college student educators can partner with this generation of college students to guide them in their journey. Entering into "learning partnerships" allows educators and students to coconstruct mutually beneficial relationships where each is empowered in the learning process (Baxter Magolda & King, 2004). This notion is especially salient as it relates to technology, because educators and older adults are often learning to navigate digital environments at the same time they try to help college students navigate them. In a learning partnership with students, educators can help college students by providing life wisdom to students navigating choices online and examining the consequences of online decisions. Students, in turn, can help educate the educators by sharing what technologies students are using, how these technologies can be used, and what affordances these technologies enable.

There are a number of strategies educators can engage in to remain current. Reading and consuming news about technological trends and youth culture ensures one can stay abreast of a rapidly changing landscape. Another, and perhaps the best source for this information, comes from the students themselves. Asking students what technologies they are using, how and why they are using it, and seeking help in navigating and experimenting with new technologies can greatly increase one's own technological knowledge and competence. Furthermore, the relationship one develops in a partnership with students is mutually beneficial. Through exploration, an educator has the opportunity to model appropriate questioning around technology and encourage students to think critically about how they use and consume digital and social media.

Students Need to be Aware of Their Digital Identities and the Impact of These Identities, and Manage Their Self-Presentation Online. Digital reputations, or identities, are increasingly important as social media and technology shift societal boundaries around privacy. This is particularly important when working with students who are seeking careers postgraduation. Recent statistics from Jobvite (2015), an online recruiting network that conducted surveys of human resources professionals across a cross-section of industries, found that 92% of job recruiters use social media to hire candidates and take into account a job candidate's social media profiles when making a hiring decision.

As individuals begin to possess digital identities and reputations, being aware of how they are perceived online, what information they choose to share, and their privacy rights will be increasingly important for all adults, particularly college students. Traditionally aged college students, as young adults, are at a critical point in their development where they will continue to make mistakes and actively experiment as they learn who they are and who they want to be. Educators can teach and protect students from making mistakes by encouraging students to articulate their goals and values in the online space and examine whether their actions are congruent with these goals and values. Furthermore, students need education about how digital reputations work, both online and offline, the consequences and possibilities of these reputations, and the opportunities for agency in defining these reputations.

Too often, however, many conversations addressing online behavior can be framed in a negative light (Junco, 2014). These conversations recount examples of individuals getting fired because of their social media posts, publicly shamed, or even arrested. Although these are worthy cautionary tales, there should be a balance in one's approach to discussing digital identities. The positive benefits of digital engagement include the ability to land a job, connect with social communities, and advance social good. Approaching digital identities in this way, assumes a "youth-normative" rather than an "adult-normative" lens (Junco, 2014). When educators engage students in conversations about issues of digital identity, it is important to strike a balance between the positive productive value of digital identities and the negative consequences of them.

Social and Digital Technologies Bring New Affordances and Environments that Require Modified Developmental Interventions and Responses.   Digital spaces provide new opportunities for action that were not previously possible in the physical world (Boyd, 2014). As a result of these affordances offered by technology, traditional scenarios in which college student educators find themselves may look different when social media is involved. For instance, whereas a roommate conflict might have previously resulted in a verbal or even physical fight, these conflicts may now surface and play out online as cyber bullying, and their psychological impact may be heightened. In another situation, where students may have previously written problematic racist or sexist thoughts anonymously on a bathroom wall, they may now post them to social networks where their visibility and impact may be much broader.

In many cases, the new ways in which these old problems instantiate themselves may give educators pause. Many of the strategies educators use in addressing analogous situations offline, however, are often still applicable when addressing situations involving digital contexts. For example, in the case of the roommate conflict, the opportunity for resolution still comes through having the students mediate the conflict through discourse. In the case of the problematic statements, community meetings for dialogue and discussion coupled with educational programming are still effective. Just because the situation may look different does not necessarily mean previously established interventions no longer work.

And yet, these new digital contexts do represent new challenges to the college student educator. Appropriate interventions require a reliance

NEW DIRECTIONS FOR STUDENT SERVICES • DOI: 10.1002/ss

on traditional methods as well as discussion about how these apply in digital spaces where the affordances and environments may be different. Case studies and dialogue with professionals are key to staying abreast of how technology is changing student behavior and can be useful tools in working through how to approach novel technological twists on traditional situations.

Developmental Theory Needs to be Applied in Online Contexts with an Appreciation of New Realities and Possibilities Existing in Online Spaces.   Although technology may be presenting educators with new scenarios and new behaviors within the online space, many of these behaviors can still be understood within the framework of existing theories of student development. Layering existing theories over college student behavior online yields many expected consistencies with developmental patterns, such as an acute need for validation and the movement from external to internal definition. It is the new forms that these behaviors take, as well as the unexpected twists that make the application or theory seem foreign or different to the educator.

In order to be effective partners to students, educators must begin to understand and apply theory in unique ways that account for digital affordances, environments, and behaviors. For example, one might investigate how theory can be applied to a student that has physical world identities that are different from their online identities. One might also explore how theory can be applied to digital environments that are more public and have reach beyond the borders of a physical world campus. Finally, one might inquire how theory may be applied to digital behaviors (such as cyberbullying) that mirror their physical world equivalents, but take on different forms and have different consequences. Beyond the digital space, generational differences in how and when one came to use, navigate, and understand technologies must be accounted for in effective educational partnerships. For example, an educator and a student may use the same social network, but use it to fulfill different goals, use different features of the software, or even use the same features differently.

Beyond foundational theory, there are hints that new or revised theory may be required to capture the college student experience fully when it is saturated with social and digital media. Technology offers new avenues for action, relationships, and self-understanding that may be shifting the human experience, and yet, students are left with few guides to help them in navigating this journey. As a result, it is important for educators to remain open to the possibility that college students may be living their lives in radically different spaces with opportunities and challenges that are unique to their growth and development at this specific point in human history. This new reality that may require the revision of the assumptions upon which previously established theory was built and something that researchers are only beginning to understand.

NEW DIRECTIONS FOR STUDENT SERVICES • DOI: 10.1002/ss

Conclusion

Social media and digital technologies are impacting the ways in which college students develop and how educators approach and understand college student behavior online. This chapter explained how social media acts as a networked public, or as technologically enabled virtual community spaces, that create new environments possessing different rules and norms than their offline equivalents. Social media also gives rise to new affordances, or ways in which human beings can act and interact. After setting the stage for how digital spaces function differently than their offline world equivalents, the terms *digital identities* and *digitized development* were explained and differentiated. The former term refers to online self-presentation, something students need to be educated about, whereas the latter term refers to changes impacting a student's psychological-developmental process, something educators must understand and seek to guide.

When confronted with these new digital realities, college student educators have an opportunity to play an important role. As educational partners to college students, educators have as much to gain from the relationship as the students themselves. As it relates to technology, educators can provide guidance, help students navigate the complexities of their digital identities and reputations, and encourage developmental growth through mentorship and exploration. Students, in turn, can help educators learn about and keep pace with technological trends and the ways in which technology can be leveraged and used. Given the rapid pace of technological change, partnerships such as these, across generational lines, can help educators and students alike.

References

Ahlquist, J. (2015). *Developing digital student leaders: A mixed methods study of student leadership, identity and decision making on social media* (Doctoral dissertation). California Lutheran University, Thousand Oaks, CA.

Arnett, J. J. (2005). Emerging adulthood: Understanding the new way of coming of age. In J. J. Arnett & J. L. Tanner (Eds.), *Emerging adults in America: Coming of age in the 21st century* (pp. 85–116). Washington, DC: American Psychological Association.

Baxter Magolda, M. B. (1999). *Creating contexts for learning and self-authorship: Constructive-developmental pedagogy.* Nashville, TN: Vanderbilt University Press.

Baxter Magolda, M. B. (2001). *Making their own way: Narratives for transforming higher education to promote self-development.* Sterling, VA: Stylus.

Baxter Magolda, M., & King, P. M. (Eds.). (2004). *Learning partnerships: Theory and models of practice to educate for self-authorship.* Sterling, VA: Stylus.

Boyd, D. (2014). *It's complicated: The social lives of networked teens.* New Haven, CT: Yale University Press.

Bronfenbrenner, U. (1993). The ecology of cognitive development: Research models and fugitive findings. In R. H. Wozniak & K. W. Fischer (Eds.), *Development in context: Acting and thinking in specific environments* (pp. 3–44). Mahwah, NJ: Erlbaum.

Brown, P. G. (2016). *College students, social media, digital identities, and the digitized self* (Doctoral dissertation). Boston College, Chestnut Hill, MA.

Chickering, A. W., & Reisser, L. (1993). *Education and identity* (2nd ed.). San Francisco, CA: Jossey-Bass.

Côté, J. E. (2005). Emerging adulthood as an institutionalized moratorium: Risks and benefits to identity formation. In J. J. Arnett & J. L. Tanner (Eds.), *Emerging adults in America: Coming of age in the 21st century* (pp. 85–116). Washington, DC: American Psychological Association.

Dahlstrom, E., Walker, J. D., & Dziuban, C. (2013). The ECAR study of undergraduate students and information technology, 2013. Retrieved from https://net.educause.edu/ir/library/pdf/ERS1302/ERS1302.pdf

Dalton, J. C., & Crosby P. C. (2013, February). Digital identity: How social media are influencing student learning and development in college. *Journal of College and Character, 14*(1), 1–4. doi:10.1515/jcc-2013-0001

Eaton, P. (2015). *#Becoming: Emergent identity of college students in the digital age examined through complexivist epistemologies* (Doctoral dissertation). Louisiana State University, Baton Rouge, LA.

Facebook. (2015). Like. Retrieved from https://www.facebook.com/help/452446998120360

Gergen, K. J. (2011, January–March). The self as social construction. *Psychological Studies, 56*(1), 108–116. doi:10.1007/s12646-011-0066-1

Gismondi, A. (2015). *#CivicEngagement: An exploratory study of social media use and civic engagement among undergraduates* (Doctoral dissertation). Boston College, Chestnut Hill, MA.

Jobvite. (2015). The Jobvite recruiter nation survey. Retrieved from http://www.jobvite.com/wp-content/uploads/2015/09/jobvite_recruiter_nation_2015.pdf

Junco, R. (2012). The relationship between frequency of Facebook use, participation in Facebook activities, and student engagement. *Computers & Education, 58,* 162–171. doi:10.1016/j.compedu.2011.08.004

Junco, R. (2014). *Engaging students through social media: Evidence-based practices for use in student affairs.* San Francisco, CA: Jossey-Bass.

Kane, G. C., Alavi, M., Labianca, G., & Borgatti, S. P. (2014). What's different about social media networks? A framework and research agenda. *MIS Quarterly, 38*(1), 275–304.

Kegan, R. (1994). *In over our heads: The mental demands of modern life.* Cambridge, MA: Harvard University Press.

Majchrzak, A. (2009, March). Comment: Where is the theory in wikis? *MIS Quarterly, 33*(1), 18–20.

Martínez Alemán, A. M., & Lynk Wartman, K. (2009). *Online social networking on campus: Understanding what matters in student culture.* New York, NY: Routledge.

Patton, L. D., Renn, K. A., Guido, F. M., & Quaye, S. J. (2016). *Student development in college: Theory, research, and practice* (3rd ed.). San Francisco, CA: Jossey-Bass.

Pempek, T. A., Yermolayeva, Y. A., & Calvert, S. L. (2009). College students' social networking experiences on Facebook. *Journal of Applied Developmental Psychology, 30,* 227–238.

Perrin, A., & Duggan, M. (2015, June 26). American internet access: 2000–2015. Retrieved from http://www.pewinternet.org/files/2015/06/2015-06-26_internet-usage-across-demographics-discover_FINAL.pdf

Prensky, M. (2001, September/October). Digital natives, digital immigrants. *On the Horizon, 9*(5), 1–5. doi:10.1108/10748120110424816

Qualman, E. (2015). *What happens on campus stays on YouTube.* Cambridge, MA: Equalman Studios.

Seider, S., & Gardner, H. (2009, April). The fragmented generation. *Journal of College & Character, 10*(4), 1–4.

Smith, A., Rainie, L., & Zickuhr, K. (2011, July 19). College students and technology. Retrieved from http://www.pewinternet.org/Reports/2011/College-students-and-technology/Report.aspx

Turkle, S. (2004, January 30). How computers change the way we think. The *Chronicle of Higher Education*. Retrieved from http://chronicle.com/article/How-Computers-Change-the-Way/10192/

PAUL GORDON BROWN is the Director of Curriculum, Training, and Research for the educational technology company, Roompact, and is an independent speaker and consultant on technology's impact on college student learning and development.

5

This chapter suggests strategies and tools for student affairs professionals to leverage digital data to measure student engagement and learning outcomes, and refine programs that enhance institutional reputation and improve student persistence. The construct of student engagement is traced from its theoretical origins to recent research connecting it to social media use.

Student Engagement Through Digital Data

Liz Gross, Jason L. Meriwether

Introduction

Over the last decade, the term *engagement* has become a digital descriptor. Offline involvement and engagement, based on work from Astin (1993), Kuh (2001), and Tinto (1987), has been the focus of many student affairs professionals, whose chief concern was the amount of time and energy students dedicated to their college experiences (Astin, 1993). This foundational work influenced the profession so much that we often use the terms *engagement* and *involvement* interchangeably, in ways not intended by the original theorists (Wolfe-Wendel, Ward, & Kinzie, 2009). Engagement in the digital age is often thought of in terms of Facebook likes, Twitter retweets, or Instagram comments. Professionals in many industries— including student affairs—have become more concerned with their engagement rate, a reference to the percentage of social media followers that interact with online content. This is not surprising, as social media use among adults has increased by nearly a factor of 10 in the last decade (Perrin, 2015). College student educators may be tempted to accept the modern, social media-influenced concept of engagement as a replacement for the traditional construct of student engagement or involvement; however, this would be shortsighted. In this chapter, we propose a comprehensive framework to assist student affairs professionals with digital data collection and analysis as they continue to evolve their digital engagement efforts.

For technologically competent student affairs professionals, both online and offline concepts of engagement may be effectively combined to provide a more comprehensive picture of a student's college experience. Most students are now experiencing college both online and offline. College students are high-frequency users of social media (Duggan, Ellison, Lampe, Lenhart, & Madden, 2015) and they report being willing

NEW DIRECTIONS FOR STUDENT SERVICES, no. 155, Autumn 2016 © 2016 Wiley Periodicals, Inc.
Published online in Wiley Online Library (wileyonlinelibrary.com) • DOI: 10.1002/ss.20184

to communicate digitally on campus (National Survey of Student Engagement [NSSE], 2014), even with faculty (Gross, 2015). To measure and assess all aspects of student engagement effectively, an understanding of digital data, including what they are, how to collect them, and how to use them to refine institutional programs, is required. In this chapter, we review the traditional construct of student engagement and related research that has attempted to integrate digital components. Then, we dive into digital data sources that may provide indicators of student engagement or an assessment of campus/department's efforts to engage their students in the digital space. Finally, we discuss how to use digital data to inform your institution's initiatives, both online and offline.

Student Engagement and Involvement

Over 50 years of research support the idea that student engagement, the amount of time and energy that students spend on activities that are deemed to have an impact on college outcomes (that is, student–faculty interaction, out-of-class course discussion, interaction with diverse individuals, involvement in student activities), and student involvement, the amount of time and energy students devote to the college experience, are predictive of important college outcomes, such as degree completion, GPA, and enrollment in graduate school (Astin, 1993; Kuh, 2003; Pascarella & Terenzini, 2005). From this point forward, we will be using the term *engagement* to refer to the activities students participate in while they are on campus. We make this choice because in student affairs, engagement is often a result of both student and institutional effort (campus-sponsored activities and programs). Additionally, Astin himself—after coining the term *student involvement*—and Tinto (1987) stated that they do not believe there are major differences between the two terms (Wolf-Wendel et al., 2009).

Research and Theory.   The roots of student engagement research and theory can be traced to Alexander Astin. In 1977, he published *Four Critical Years*, a seminal examination of the impact of college on a variety of student outcomes based on longitudinal data from five large samples of freshmen in the 1960s. Almost a decade later, Astin (1993) published a follow-up, entitled *What Matters in College: Four Critical Years Revisited*, based on the class of 1989. Astin conceptualized five categories of student involvement: academic, faculty, peer, work, and other. Activities falling within all of these categories are the purview of student affairs professionals, such as peer interaction, volunteering, part-time campus jobs, internships, intramural sports, and tutoring.

Tinto (1987) contributed to the scholarship of student engagement with his theory of student departure. He proposed that the ability of a student to integrate into campus life (in addition to interacting with faculty) directly influenced whether or not the student would remain on campus until graduation. In his recent work, Tinto (2006) called for additional research to determine how to drive engagement in different settings and with students that fall outside the norm of young, residential students who were the subject of most research in the past. Conducting additional research in this area requires student affairs professionals and scholars with highly developed technology competency to consider how digital engagement data can be used in this context.

Pascarella and Terenzini (2005) spent decades evaluating studies related to student activities and college outcomes. The most valuable peer interaction happens when students engage with other students who are different from them and cause them to consider a variety of perspectives that are different from their own. They make the bold statement that "interaction with peers is probably the most pervasive and powerful force in student persistence and degree completion" (Pascarella & Terenzini, 2005, p. 615).

With these robust data in hand, student affairs professionals have evidence to support efforts to encourage peer interaction among students in person, as well as specific co-curricular activities on campus. As personal technology use and online media have increased over the last decade, researchers are investigating whether technology influences student behavior, and if certain online activities contribute to student engagement.

Measuring Student Engagement. At the turn of the century, George Kuh began studying student engagement, largely through the administration of the National Survey of Student Engagement (NSSE) (Kuh, 2001, 2003). Continuing the earlier research of Astin, Pascarella, Terenzini, and others, the NSSE seeks to quantify student engagement by measuring variables shown to correlate with desired college outcomes positively. Specifically, the NSSE measures five benchmarks: level of academic challenge, student–faculty interaction, active and collaborative learning, enriching educational experiences, and supportive campus environment (Kuh, 2003).

The NSSE did not specifically inquire about technology until 2003, where the questions focused largely on student–faculty interaction. Students were asked a variety of technology-related questions, including how often their instructors required them to use technology, how often they communicated with students online about academic matters, if they collaborated using technology, or e-mailed instructors. The majority of students reported that instructors required them to use technology in their courses, and more than half of students reported communicating frequently with their peers online for academic purposes. Laird and Kuh (2005) analyzed 2003 NSSE data, and after controlling for demographic and collegiate experience characteristics, found a moderate correlation between using information technology for academic purposes and student–faculty interaction. A deeper analysis of the data led Laird and Kuh (2005) to question whether use of technology is a contributing factor to the already-established dimensions of student engagement measured by NSSE, or an additional factor warranting further explanation. This question, however, does not appear to have been examined in analysis of NSSE data over the following decade.

NEW DIRECTIONS FOR STUDENT SERVICES • DOI: 10.1002/ss

Social Media and Student Engagement. The 2014 administration of the NSSE included a set of experimental items with the survey administration at 44 campuses. These items sought to determine the relationship between social media use and various components of student engagement, including out-of-class activities. The survey instrument focused on two specific uses of social media: learning-directed and distracted. NSSE (2014) defined learning-directed uses of social media as "understanding course materials and ideas; learning, studying, or completing coursework with other students; connecting to people who are different in terms of race, social class, religion, or political beliefs; and understanding controversial issues from multiple perspectives" (p. 16). Distracted uses of social media are defined as "distracting students from completing coursework, paying attention in class, participating in campus events and social activities, or doing group work with other students; as well as feeling intimidated by other students" (NSSE, 2014, p. 16). Learning-directed uses of social media are positively correlated with 10 engagement indicators, including reflective and integrative learning, collaborative learning, discussions with diverse others, and supportive environment. Over half of first-year students reported that their campus was using social media to help them connect with other students and campus organizations.

Junco (2014) conducted original research and a literature review to determine the relationship between Facebook and student engagement. Particular uses of Facebook such as creating or responding to events, commenting, or viewing photos (Junco, 2011)—rather than simple use versus nonuse—are related to student engagement as defined by Astin (1993) and Kuh (2003), and also appear to contribute to academic and social integration as defined by Tinto (1987). Junco noted that this is the case without any direction from campus faculty or staff, and posited that student affairs professionals could direct students to particular uses that would further impact positive college outcomes. For example, to deepen individual relationships with students, professionals can engage in social listening (monitoring social media for key terms like campus and office names, often on Twitter) in order to respond to students that express concerns about a department rather than to a department. To engage in community building, campuses and departments can utilize Facebook groups and hashtags on Instagram or Twitter to connect students with comment interests and experiences. A popular strategy is to include a class hashtag with acceptance materials so incoming students can connect with each other before they get to campus for orientation (Junco, 2014). Gross (2015) also suggested that a multichannel communication strategy, including social media and text messaging, could increase instances of student–faculty interaction, specifically about the topics that contribute to student engagement.

Students are using social media and other technology to participate in the college experience, including activities that contribute to student engagement. The remainder of this chapter will help student affairs

New Directions for Student Services • DOI: 10.1002/ss

professionals collect and analyze data about the specific ways students are using social media and other digital technology to participate in activities that contribute to student engagement, and then to use the results to improve campus programming.

Collecting and Assessing Digital Data

For the purposes of this chapter, digital data reflect student behavior, attitudes, demographics, opinions, and experience; they exist in electronic form and can be accessed or downloaded for analysis. The data may or may not be generated by online activities; in fact, often, online data are simply a digital record of offline behavior. For example, students post photos on Instagram depicting what they did over the weekend. The Instagram photos and associated hashtags are digital data, but they are describing offline behavior. Digital data sources include campus customer relationship management systems (CRMs), social media, card-swipe records, online student assessments, student-authored blog posts, and other sources that will likely become available between the writing and publishing of this chapter.

Types of Digital Data.   Digital data exist in three distinct forms: individual, aggregate, and metadata. All three forms of data can be quantitative or qualitative, but all three may not be available depending on your data source. Individual data include statements made by a single person in a digital space such as

- A tweet or Facebook post
- Individual activity records such as attendance at campus events tracked by an identification card swipe system
- Total number of Twitter posts made by a single account
- Characteristics included in an individual's online profile, such as demographics and descriptive information.

Although individual data most often provide a window into the student experience, they can alert campuses to potential problems, ranging from the easily fixable—a Facebook post about a subpar experience in campus housing (Berkman, 2013)—to anonymous threats of campus violence on YikYak (Alcindor & Stanglin, 2015).

Aggregate data combine data from multiple individuals into one data source. Aggregate data may include the complete record of statements made about a particular topic, such as the search results for a Twitter hashtag, the activity stats of a group of individuals such as Facebook Page data, Twitter Analytics, engagement statistics from admitted students logged in the campus CRM, data collected from a sample such as Skyfactor or other campus survey data, and sentiment data from public social media posts mentioning the name of your campus. Nekritz (2015) highlighted how he used Topsy to track all uses of the #WhyIChoseOswego hashtag on decision day, and loosely correlated it with an increase in admissions deposits. Indiana State University used aggregate data from Skyfactor to identify the top five issues within the first-year cohort, including homesickness and test anxiety, and designed interventions to address these issues (Peck, 2013).

Metadata are data about data. It can tell you how, when, and where data were created. Examples of metadata include location tagging, time stamps, and sources such as device type, operating system, and application name. Users of Instagram, for example, can search for posts by location from any place in the world—including college campuses they attend or are considering attending (Instagram, n.d.). The University of South Carolina utilizes location data to display the wide-reaching geography of students who shared their acceptance on Instagram with the hashtag #UofSCYES from coast to coast (Ditty, 2015).

Ethics of Digital Data Collection and Analysis. Students are creating hundreds, if not thousands, of pieces of digital data related to their campus experience every day, and some of these data are available publicly. Research from as early as 2009 indicates that college students are savvy social media users and are confident in the ability to adjust their privacy settings and regularly do so (Boyd & Hargittai, 2010). However, it is nearly impossible for student affairs practitioners or researchers to obtain informed consent from the creators of public digital data. What matters most often in this situation is context (Gleibs, 2014). If students create digital data intending for their data to be public, such as by using the hashtag for an event or posting publicly to a campus Facebook page, the use of such data for analysis poses little, if any concern. If, however, the data came from a private Facebook group or an individual exchange between friends, intention and the context is not clear and should be considered before proceeding with analysis.

Some campuses are beginning to address this issue by including social media policies in their student handbooks. The University of Memphis Fogelman College of Business and Economics states in its student social media policy, "realize that information you post without using appropriate privacy settings may be available to anyone including University and College faculty, current or prospective employers, graduate school admissions officers, and many more" (University of Memphis, n.d., paragraph 2). San Jacinto College clearly states on its Web site that it monitors public social media posts that include the name of the campus and that students could be subject to disciplinary action based on those posts (San Jacinto College, n.d.)

Another ethical consideration when using publicly available digital data is the use of personally identifying information that accompanies online posts. Often, it may be helpful for student affairs professionals to provide examples of the data they've encountered (for example, tweets, Facebook posts, Tumblr entries) when sharing their assessment with stakeholders. In all cases, removing names and usernames and blurring profile photos should protect personal anonymity. Given the highly searchable nature of social networks, such as Twitter, Facebook, and Tumblr, posts should also be summarized, rather than shared verbatim. This is because the text of a post has been indexed by search engines and could easily be traced back to the user (Rivers & Lewis, 2014).

Measuring Social Media Activity—Account Based. Over half of first-year students report that their campus uses social media to connect them to campus activities or their peers (NSSE, 2014). Often, this is done through a campus or departmental page on Facebook, Twitter, Instagram, or another social network. If a department maintains an account on any of the popular social media platforms, it is likely that the department has access to data about the number of people that "follow" or "like" the account, some of their demographic characteristics, how many people see posts, and how they interact with them. This information is referred to as social media analytics, and can help determine how students are utilizing the accounts departments created. Erika Fields, former Web content and communications director for the Center for Work and Service at Wellesley College, used account-based data to determine how best to promote career development and service learning events (personal communication, November 11, 2015. After tracking interactions on Facebook and Twitter posts that promoted the events, as well as RSVPs received from e-mail and the online information portal, she was able to document that students were much more likely to respond to event invitations sent via e-mail. This finding allows her to focus her event marketing resources on e-mail, rather than social media. However, Facebook data also helped Erika understand that students do interact with posts from her office on Facebook—they were just much less likely to interact with Facebook events. Rather, they're most likely to read, share, and comment on stories about what students have done with their Wellesley degree or stories that inspire achievement and shed light on campus opportunities for engagement (E. Fields, personal communication, November 11, 2015).

If social media is part of a departmental or divisional student engagement strategy, collecting these data about the performance of these social media efforts is paramount. It is important to take some time to examine the objectives or learning outcomes of an area's social media program and then determine what data best measure progress toward those objectives or outcomes. Some guiding questions and metrics include:

- If the goal is to get content in front of students, reach/impressions (that is, the number of people who see a post) may be a good metric.
- If the goal is to spark conversation, likes/comments/share/retweets (collectively, engagement rate) are the metrics on which staff should focus.
- If the target audience is prospective, traditional-aged students, an analysis of audience demographics may tell staff if the department is connecting with the right types of people.

- If the social media efforts are intended to drive traffic to a campus Web site, staff members will want to focus on link clicks.
- If Web visits are then meant to result in an action such as completing a form, signing up for an event), non–social-media data (for example, Web analytics) may be necessary. Those data are beyond the scope of this chapter, but should be explored if a campus or department is using social media to promote specific actions on a Web site. Google offers free training through their Analytics Academy and staff can find great resources specific to higher education at www.higheredanalytics.com and www.collegewebeditor.com.

Finding and Analyzing Public Online Posts.   Much of the online activity that your students participate in is public, including blog posts, public tweets, or YouTube videos. If students choose not to apply privacy filters to their posts, they may be found, searched, and analyzed. These data offer student affairs professionals a chance to learn more about their student's authentic experience. For example, admissions staff may learn more about what prospective students are saying about their college search, how they felt about a campus tour, or what other campuses they are considering. Additionally, campus activities staff can learn more about the student experience, what activities generate online chatter, and how students are adjusting to college. Furthermore, campus auxiliaries can gather valuable, unfiltered data about service levels of housing, dining, or the student union. Student affairs educators have a unique ability to understand students' perspectives from their residence hall room or on the campus sidewalk by analyzing these public online data.

Although the Twitter database is easily searchable without a third-party tool, effectively searching the social Web for all mentions of a campus, department, or program will likely require specialized social media listening/monitoring software. Some examples include Sprout Social, Spredfast, Salesforce Marketing Cloud, Brandwatch, Meltwater Buzz, and Sysomos Heartbeat. All of these examples are offered at a variety of price points, allowing users to create complex queries that combine keywords with Boolean logic to search the social Web and return results about a specific topic. Boolean logic includes the use of operators, such as AND, OR, and NOT to create more sophisticated queries and is essential in order to search for specific instances of general terms.

Once search results are identified, the following types of analysis can be conducted. Sentiment (qualitative), which helps describe if a conversation is trending positive or negative; frequency (quantitative), which clearly indicates how many mentions of a particular topic have occurred within a finite time frame; keyword analysis (qualitative), which scans the text for every mention and surfaces the most-often-used words, and source (quantitative), which scans the metadata and determines what network was used to post the mention. Some software also allows analysis of the demographics of the people who posted messages (assuming they included that information in their social media profile). Depending on specific needs, compiling some or all of these analyses into a summary report could provide campus decision makers with the information they need to understand the "pulse" of campus life.

Collecting Digital Data from Campus-Based Systems

A cohesive research and assessment strategy can combine data from multiple systems used across campus—even outside of student affairs. Marketing response data, Web analytics, and student activity data can provide a robust description of student engagement. When examined independently, specific populations that have potential for increased engagement can be identified in order to pilot new or altered strategies.

Integrating Social Media Outreach Through Digital Targeting. Many institutions take advantage of digital targeting to communicate with potential students—providing marketing and recruitment messages or promoting campus events. Examples include purchasing space through forums such as Facebook or Twitter that targets certain IP addresses. Based on strategic priorities, any university can purchase sponsored advertisements, which appear in social media feeds within certain zip codes or targeted areas. Figure 5.1 is a sample of a digitally targeted advertisement that lands on Facebook, Twitter, Instagram, and Pandora within certain recruitment markets for Indiana University Southeast.

Although capturing increased Web site views is a simple way to measure impact of digital targeting, there are more robust measures that are ideal for demonstrating effectiveness. According to Laird and Kuh (2005), adequately planning measurement can help to predict outcomes, which could be helpful as social media initiatives are developed. For example, Junco (2014) noted that with social media, "we have tangible evidence of how many students participate in the intervention, the level at which they participate, and whether they continue to participate" (p. 210). Meriwether (2015) suggested ensuring that effective expression of measurable outcomes must include a demonstrated impact on learning, a quantifiable increase in engagement or student activity, and quantitative measurements of responsiveness.

Figure 5.1. Example of a digitally targeted advertisement for recruitment through social media sites.

Figure 5.2. Sample mobile friendly recruitment Web page.

When planning a social media engagement strategy such as digital targeting, Junco (2014) recommended 10 implementation steps for consideration, 5 of which are particularly relevant to digital targeting, and include:

1. Defining populations for targeting
2. Selecting appropriate social media platforms
3. Planning appropriate content for engagement
4. Assigning responsibility for engaging with students
5. Continuity of platform use following the social media intervention

For example, to reach students who demonstrate a preference for communication through digital means or via social media, student affairs leaders can leverage their campus CRM system to initiate and send digital and social media messages. Utilizing the campus CRM software also allows for direct tracking of engagement, measuring student responsiveness, demonstrating yield, and relative ease to compare variables within a plethora of academic and co-curricular contexts. Figure 5.2 below demonstrates a mobile-friendly landing page that can capture information of potential students and allows their involvement in campus activities, digital engagement, and academic performance to be tracked upon enrollment.

Measuring Student Success Through Curricular Involvement and Social Media.   Measuring student engagement and academic performance is an effective way of collecting data to demonstrate outcomes. Understanding and capturing measurable outcomes from each of the sources described earlier also provides data that can be used for predicting student performance, identifying elements of the campus experience that enhance student perpetuity, and identifying barriers to success. For example, tracking trends

NEW DIRECTIONS FOR STUDENT SERVICES • DOI: 10.1002/ss

in recreation center use can occur by capturing swipes of the student identification card. Student engagement can also be captured through software systems, such as Check I'm Here, CollegiateLink, or OrgSync, which can be funneled into a cocurricular transcript. Assessing academic performance of students in relation to co-curricular activities, such as internships, student government, fraternity or sorority affiliation, community service, or service learning, can lead to significant findings when compared to noninvolved students. Indices for students across academic majors can also be a variable for comparison and analysis.

Accordingly, another measurable variable among these student populations is social media use. Studies can capture data for students who engage social media in classroom learning, or through engagement interventions through student affairs. These variables provide a myriad of academic performance comparisons across groups based on levels of engagement and social media activity academic and co-curricular settings. Further, categories for digital engagement can be developed for inclusion in co-curricular transcripts. Longitudinally, these students can also be tracked after graduation to measure employment outcomes, graduate school placement and outcomes, or alumni giving. Following the implementation of one or more strategies described above, it is important to develop a system that provides easy access to the large amount of data collected.

Implementing Automated Reporting Systems

Automated reporting, the process of generating data reports to provide information at set points in a cycle of an ongoing strategy, is a valuable tool to manage data collected through digital targeting, as well as efforts to support student persistence through curricular or co-curricular social media engagement. Junco (2014) suggested collaborating with assessment professionals in student affairs or institutional research to leverage their expertise in analyzing data. By collaborating with the appropriate stakeholders, student affairs professionals can establish automated reports that capture trends and allow for updates to reflect various points-in-cycle for comparison and analysis. Such reporting can occur at any time, such as prior to midterms, weekly, or even once monthly, depending on organizational needs. For example, automated reports allow real-time snapshots of data at any useful level of frequency. The impact of automated reports is greatest when comparative data are established that compare to prior points-in-cycle, or even to national trends for social media engagement. Some institutions may compare student retention data for students who were targeted for a digital campaign and design an automated report to capture the retention trend for the same population the year before the strategy was initiated. The data can demonstrate effectiveness or ineffectiveness of the strategy.

Other examples of leveraging automated reporting include tracking cohorts, or control groups, or groups within certain variables of

NEW DIRECTIONS FOR STUDENT SERVICES • DOI: 10.1002/ss

measurement to track programmatic data, co-curricular activities, and outcomes for digital targeting campaigns. Describing automated reporting, Meriwether (2013) explained the value of leveraging such systems, noting that student affairs professionals "can all empower our teams with strategic and intentional systems that guide our processes, track our metrics, and inform our decisions" (paragraph 5). For example, student affairs teams can track a group of students who participate in a summer precollege program to measure their program participation, academic performance, and organizational involvement during the first year. The reports can run automatically over any assigned time period, and be designed to compare outcomes for students in the summer program in contrast to other student populations at many given points during the academic year. Such reporting can generate real-time data that demonstrate program effectiveness and student learning, and provide outcomes reporting for senior student affairs officers or other university stakeholders.

Using Social Media Outcomes to Inform Student Affairs Initiatives

The path to leveraging digital tools and social media effectively among faculty or institutional leaders requires a specific plan tied to measurement, assessment, and most of all, a clear path to student learning. Accordingly, we will outline a few strategies to help launch and maintain a robust and effective social media initiative in student affairs.

Mitigate Reticence With Data and Measurable Outcomes. Reticence to supporting digital media efforts may be fueled by fear that an inaccurate, opinion-based, or incorrect post could lead to backlash for one's self or the university. It is important that student affairs professionals capture data that demonstrate student consumption of digital media. Although familiarity with national trends is important, measuring digital and social media consumption among current students on a given campus could be effective tools for discussion with colleagues who are resistant to social media. By measuring and demonstrating digital consumption trends, professionals are more empowered to inform how digital tools can impact marketing, branding, and reputations of a student affairs division, or the entire university.

Begin With the Brand. University marketing departments are excellent resources to develop a digital identity and find content for posting that is congruent with the campus mission and vision for student affairs. These partnerships can also ensure that university policies and guidelines are followed, and that the student affairs digital brand is consistent with institutional voice (Cabellon, 2010; Junco, 2014). Collaborating with these stakeholders will help student affairs professionals frame their approach to digital media in a way that is consistent with the university branding strategy, which could be more readily accepted by senior student affairs officers or supervisors who are less familiar with digital media.

Start With Your Students. Hiring social-media–savvy students among graduate assistants, student leaders, or majors in relevant programs can provide a wealth of resources for student affairs professionals seeking to plant a digital flag for their departments or divisions. It may also be a great way to learn the nuances and locations of your students' digital hangouts. Cabellon (2015) also described the use of student employees from academic programs such as graphic design, business, or communication, who operate as a team to implement the digital engagement model at his university. Critical to such an approach, however, is to implement a robust training experience for participants.

Defuse Student Complaints. Understanding the student digital community exceeds simply tracking numbers to recognize trends (Lewis & Rush, 2013). These insights are particularly useful as tools when students use social media to lodge complaints or direct comments that have little factual basis. In such cases, student affairs leaders should eschew a digital duel online. A brief response that offers a hyperlink or quote of a specific policy or statement is often a more suitable approach than trying to argue about a point of view. There is little room for clearing up context over a social media forum, which often calls for shorter and more fact-based responses. Additionally, other viewers to the exchange can become more focused on interpreting the words of the administrator than on reading the information that is valuable to the argument. Defusing an argumentative post with a cited policy or data point can be an effective strategy. Additionally, it is important to offer an option for the online complainant to contact the person on staff who can best assist offline. Offering to set up an appointment with the student and the appropriate affairs leader is a defusion technique that can prevent response to the original complaint from escalating into a public debate or spectacle. Explaining that other students have asked the same specific question or sharing that the information provided was presented to students in another digital or in-person forum are also effective tools to defuse online conflict. The direct engagement of student concerns on social media can lead to meaningful long-term relationships between professionals and students and enhance credibility of the student affairs department or division.

Conclusion

This chapter provides strategies to leverage digital tools to recruit students, and to understand and demonstrate student engagement on campus. Leaders in student affairs can utilize these strategies to initiate and secure campus partnerships, to capture and analyze data, and to articulate measurable outcomes from digital and social media interventions clearly. Junco (2014) expounded on the pressure to deliver results with respect to social media, noting, "skepticism about the value of social media in students' lives support the need to assess how what we do with our students both off and on social media has an impact on their learning developmental outcomes" (p. 239). The ability to use social media and other digital data as viable elements of the student experience allows student affairs professionals to communicate measurable outcomes. By expanding the context, methodology, and lexicon through which social media and digital tools are explained, student affairs professionals will be in a stronger position to share outcomes that are easily understood, clear to decision-makers, and most importantly, accepted by colleagues in the academy and across the institution.

References

Alcindor, Y., & Stanglin, D. (2015, November 11). 2 suspects arrested in social media threats at Missouri campus. *USA Today.* Retrieved from http://www.usatoday.com/story/news/2015/11/11/some-at-u-of-missouri-on-edge-after-social-media-threats-of-violence/75559034/

Astin, A. W. (1977). *Four critical years: Effects of college on beliefs, attitudes and knowledge.* San Francisco, CA: Jossey-Bass.

Astin, A. W. (1993). *What matters in college? Four critical years revisited.* San Francisco, CA: Jossey-Bass.

Berkman, F. (2013, August 20). Facebook page shames university's revolting dorm rooms. Mashable. Retrieved from http://mashable.com/2013/08/20/facebook-shames-gwu/

Boyd, D., & Hargittai, E. (2010). Facebook privacy settings: Who cares? *First Monday, 15*(8). Retrieved from http://firstmonday.org/ojs/index.php/fm/article/view/3086/2589

Cabellon, E. (2010). A student affairs social media plan [Web log post]. Retrieved from http://edcabellon.com/tech/socialmediaplan/

Cabellon, E. (2015). A student affairs integrated communication strategy [Web log post]. Retrieved from http://edcabellon.com/interests/studentaffairscommunicationstrategy/

Ditty, A. (2015, May 12). How higher education does instagram marketing [Web log post]. Retrieved from: http://blog.seenmoment.com/how-higher-education-does-instagram-marketing

Duggan, M., Ellison, N., Lampe, C., Lenhart, A., & Madden, M. (2015). *Social media update 2014.* Washington, DC: Pew Internet & American Life Project.

Gleibs, I.H. (2014). Turning virtual public spaces into laboratories: Thoughts on conducting online field studies using social network sites. *Analyses of Social Issues and Public Policy, 14*(1), 352–370.

Gross, L. (2015). *An examination of the relationship between the communication methods used in out-of-class student-faculty interactions and the content and frequency of those interactions* (Doctoral dissertation). Cardinal Stritch University, Milwaukee, WI.

Instagram. (n.d.). The all-new search and explore: See the world as it happens [Web log post]. Retrieved from: http://blog.instagram.com/post/122260662827/150623-search-and-explore

Junco, R. (2011, August 22). Time spent on Facebook is related to involvement in campus activities [Web log post]. Retrieved from: http://blog.reyjunco.com/time-spent-on-facebook-is-related-to-involvement-in-campus-activities

Junco, R. (2014). *Engaging students through social media: Evidence-based practices for use in student affairs.* San Francisco, CA: Jossey-Bass.

Kuh, G. D. (2001). Assessing what really matters in student learning. *Change. The Magazine of Higher Learning, 33*(3), 10–17.

Kuh, G. D. (2003). What we're learning about student engagement from the NSSE. *Change: The Magazine of Higher Learning, 35*(2), 24–32.

Laird, T. F., & Kuh, G. D. (2005). Student experiences with information technology and their relationship to other aspects of student engagement. *Research in Higher Education, 46*(2), 211–233. doi: 10.1007/s 11162–004–1600-y

Lewis, B., & Rush, D. (2013). Experience of developing twitter-based communities of practice in higher education. *Research in Learning Technology, 21*, 1–35.

Meriwether, J. L. (2013, November 26). Automated reporting: The simple answer for the consistent questions [Web log post]. Retrieved from http://www.naspa.org/constituent-groups/posts/automated-reporting-the-simple-answer-for-the-consistent-questions

Meriwether, J. L. (2015, September). Creating a collaborative student affairs social media strategy [Web log post]. Retrieved from http://www.socialnomics.net/2015/08/31/creating-a-collaborative-student-affairs-social-media-strategy/

National Survey of Student Engagement. (NSSE). (2014). *Bringing the institution into focus annual results 2014.* Bloomington, IN: Indiana University Center for Postsecondary Research.

Nekritz, T. (2015). #whyichoseoswego: a quick and lovely user-generated success story. Retrieved from: https://insidetimshead.wordpress.com/2015/05/06/whyichoseoswego-a-quick-and-lovely-user-generated-success-story/

Pascarella, E. T., & Terenzini, P. T. (2005). *How college affects students: A third decade of research.* San Francisco, CA: Jossey-Bass.

Peck, L. (2013). Creating a culture of success using Map-Works. Presented at the Student Success Conference, Terre Haute, Indiana. Retrieved from: http://www2.indstate.edu/studentsuccess/pdf/Conference%20presentations/Session2—MAP-works%20SSC%20Powerpoint.pdf

Perrin, A. (2015). *Social media usage: 2005–2015.* Washington, DC: Pew Internet & American Life Project.

Rivers, C. M., & Lewis, B. L. (2014). Ethical research standards in a world of big data [version1; referees:2 approved with reservations]. *F1000Research, 3*(38). doi: 10.12688/f100research.3-38.v2

San Jacinto College. (n.d.). Students and social media. Retrieved from: http://www.sanjac.edu/about-san-jac/college-operations/marketing-pr-and-govt-affairs/social-media/social-media-student

Tinto, V. (1987). *Leaving college: Rethinking the causes and cures of student attrition.* Chicago, IL: University of Chicago Press.

Tinto, V. (2006). Research and practice of student retention: What's next?. *Journal of College Student Retention, 8*(1), 1–19.

University of Memphis. (n.d.). Social networking guidelines. Retrieved from http://www.memphis.edu/fcbe/pdfs/about/social_media_guidelines_students.pdf

Wolfe-Wendel, K., Ward, K., & Kinzie, J. (2009). A tangled web of terms: The overlap and unique contribution of involvement, engagement, and integration to understanding student success. *Journal of College Student Development, 50*(4), 407–428.

LIZ GROSS *is a higher education professional currently working as a social media and market research strategist for a federal student loan servicer.*

JASON L. MERIWETHER *is the vice chancellor for student affairs and enrollment management at Indiana University Southeast and a social media and higher education blogger for Socialnomics.net.*

NEW DIRECTIONS FOR STUDENT SERVICES • DOI: 10.1002/ss

This chapter describes how to establish social media guidelines and policies for colleges and universities effectively, based upon a field study of postsecondary education institutions representing 10 different countries. To further community interactions and social media involvement, this chapter will outline effective practical approaches for the creation and implementation of policy and guidance in higher education.

Setting the Course: Strategies for Writing Digital and Social Guidelines

Laura A. Pasquini

Social media use in higher education is steadily becoming a conventional practice among institutional stakeholders, including students, staff, and faculty (Wang & Meiselwitz, 2015). Characteristically, these social media applications are networked, primarily free, and organic in nature driven by the creation and exchange of user-generated content (Kaplan & Haenlein, 2010). The social web allows for interactivity for users to connect with each other, gather news and information, create content, and share openly. A growing number of colleges and universities are connecting with students, faculty, staff, and alumni to enhance institutional processes, open communication channels, and enrich campus involvement. Computer-mediated tools, like social media, provide higher education stakeholders with venues to participate, interact, and monitor communication discourse (Blaschke, 2014). On campuses today, both information-sharing and digital networks create authentic openings for collaborative practices, online interactions, and individualized learning experiences (Smith, 2013). In turn, colleges and universities are cognizant that social and emerging technologies influence and impact all campus stakeholders. Social media provides campus communities with a number of affordances; however, at the same time, higher education stakeholders struggle with how to manage behaviors and use on these channels that are not governed by current policies and practices. Social media channels are organic, and are typically not considered part of the "official" institutional technology landscape. Increasingly, colleges and universities are faced with questions, incidents, and challenges surrounding social media, so many are considering how to develop standards and protocols for use effectively. Because of the popularity and broad

NEW DIRECTIONS FOR STUDENT SERVICES, no. 155, Autumn 2016 © 2016 Wiley Periodicals, Inc.
Published online in Wiley Online Library (wileyonlinelibrary.com) • DOI: 10.1002/ss.20185

use of the social Web, both administrators and educators are concerned about challenges and how to best direct this tool.

The higher education sector has witnessed a number of events influenced by social media, including digital attacks on senior administration (Holloway & Boccelli, 2014), infringements of academic freedom rights (Salaita, 2015), inappropriate online professional behavior (Thomason, 2015), academic misconduct and plagiarism (Glendinning, 2014), university crisis communication (Snoeijers, Poels, & Nicolay, 2014), ethical approval of research conducted via social media (Sandvig, 2015), cyberstalking and sexual assault threats (Jouvenal & Shapiro, 2015), viral sharing of campus incidents (Kingkade, 2015), online abuse and harassment (Wile, 2015), and cyberbullying at college (Selkie, 2015). With frequent use and increased acceptance, higher education administrators need to place a high priority on developing guidelines and practices to nurture the online climate and support community development. The creation and implementation of digital governance should not only be to set protocols for social media use, it should enhance current institutional practices and behaviors impacted by these technologies. Based on findings from the Pasquini and Evangelopoulos (2015) research, this chapter outlines specific recommendations and strategies for higher education stakeholders who will steward digital and social media guidelines.

Social Media in Higher Education

Many organizations adopt social media applications for internal and external use for productivity, communication, or brand management. Hanna, Rohm, and Crittenden (2011) identified organizations that value and recognize the importance of using social media platforms; however, many rarely know how to deploy social, online spaces within their organization. For the higher education sector the primary concern for social media use is connected to privacy (Joosten, Pasquini, & Harness, 2013) and federal regulations, such as the United States Family Education Rights and Protection Act (Joosten, 2012). For social media engagement at colleges and universities, utilization and behaviors on these connected channels require guidance, direction, and support.

Postsecondary institutions are increasingly concerned about offering guidelines and policies for digital behavior to protect personal and professional reputations (Snyder, 2014), safeguard against legal implications (Scott & Jacka, 2011), and adhere to set regulations when monitoring, regulating, and disciplining users (McHale, 2012). No longer can college and university campuses overlook questions about ownership of intellectual property, legal use, identity management, and literacy development on social media (Rodriguez, 2011). Typically rules and regulations for social media use discourage participation and rarely provide learning and development opportunities, by providing guidelines, best practices, and examples of use (Joosten, 2012; Joosten et al., 2013; Junco, 2014). To manage emergent challenges and opportunities on these digital platforms effectively, social media guidance needs to consider ethical, legal, and support aspects beyond its communication and marketing function.

Social Media Governance Drafting for Higher Education

In thinking about utilizing social media platforms for engagement, learning, and community development on campus, institutional leaders should be concerned with how to govern its use. This method of governance with social media requires a fine balance between directive policies and guiding principles to trust that members of the campus community will use their common sense. To direct social media policy and establish how to draft guidelines, it is critical that higher education administrators identify planning measures that include objectives, management strategies, community building goals, and local support on campus. Effective social media policies for colleges and universities should offer comprehensive guidelines to coach institutional stakeholders, while also providing policies of what is expected for online behavior and use. Higher education administrators should consider action items such as the establishment of a social media governance and/or planning group, creating learning objects for training and development, and identifying implementation challenges for both policy and practice.

For writing social media and digital governance documents, these key content areas will continue to expand as social technologies evolve and the institutional users modify their own participation on these platforms. Campus administrators and community managers can utilize these resources as a central reference point when crafting institutional policies and guidelines; however, it is suggested that a local social media advisory group represent institutional goals and needs for campus planning. To support social media governance development at an institution, the following areas should be considered when crafting policies and/or guidelines.

Assessment, Planning, Drafting, and Support for Implementation. For the purpose of these four pillars and recommendations, the following terminology will be used to discuss social media guideline and/or policy development. The term *organizations* may be used interchangeably with higher education institutions and/or the specific department or unit who will be responsible for the social media guideline and/or policy. The terms *social media or higher education administrator* and *community manager* will be used for those individuals stewarding the social media direction within an institution. This individual might direct social media protocols, manage specific organizational accounts, support community development, and scaffold use of platforms within an institution. Finally, the terms *community* *users* or *users* will refer to institutional stakeholders, including students, staff, faculty, alumni, and campus partners.

Assessment: Advisory and Auditing.   Social media is not just about the technology; it is primarily focused on the social. Policies and guidelines create a foundation for community users to interact and participate on campus. These platforms should not be seen as another means for messaging, broadcasting, or distributing information to institutional stakeholders. Social media spaces may be thought of as a way to empower and engage the community. Consider who will help assess, review, and develop campus social media policies. This process will require consulting members of the institution's social media community to determine needs and directives for governance models.

For policy and guideline implementation to be a success, university staff must involve institutional stakeholders in the development of writing social media governance and planning for effective campus practices. Start with the campus population to understand, assess, and encourage a public discourse around acceptable standards and community expectations online. It is recommended to provide the institution with a central social media directory, as it encourages a community network and a central, accessible resource to find other social content, share relevant information, and model social media practices among social media managers.

Social Media Advisory Group.   To help organize a social media assessment, it is highly suggested to appoint and utilize the expertise from a campus social media advisory group. Social media advisory groups are typically formed to serve as the coordinating and consulting body for the campus. This working group will be established to provide continual insight for policy revision, ongoing maintenance of the guidelines, and organizational learning support based on the institution's stakeholder needs, specifically with regards to social media behavior and use. These individuals may be representative of various students, employees, and academic staff at the institution, specifically those who might already be involved on social media platforms.

The social media advisory group will serve as a consulting council or committee of institutional stakeholders who will set up and execute the resulting social media strategy, and outline guiding documents, policy adoption, and brainstorming of potential opportunities and challenges for social media use for the campus. It is essential to gain buy-in from the larger campus community when drafting social media policy and guideline documents; however, members of the social media advisory group will want to leverage institutional stakeholders who have a true passion for community and collaboration, and have an awareness of the functionality of the social media platforms. Contributions and partnerships from a variety of divisions on campus will help broaden university guidelines and take into multiple facets of the campus' policy writing needs; however, these advocates will keep the community users' interests at the core of university policy and/or

NEW DIRECTIONS FOR STUDENT SERVICES • DOI: 10.1002/ss

guideline development. The advisory group can help support research efforts by "listening" to the community interactions on campus, and determine if a social media policies and/or guidelines are effectively communicated internally (to institutional stakeholders) and externally (to campus partners) for using institutional social media platforms.

Social Media Audit. Think of social media channels as a way to empower and engage the campus community. Have you assessed what this is at the institution? Who is currently engaged online? These are typically individuals who are part of the conversation, creating content, active in institutional accounts, and often commenting on what is happening. Where are the institutional stakeholders talking? Before administrators think of the social media platform and assess the needs and interests of the current campus community online, they must ask the following questions. How do community members share and interact online? What are their preferred applications, platforms, and networks? What does the interaction look like? What patterns and trends do you see on institutional social media accounts? How can the campus cultivate community and organize ways to engage online? This first phase will require a group to conduct a social media audit to understand the institutional social media landscape. This should include a needs assessment of social media platforms on campus, specifically the currently used platforms, reviewing the conversation in networks, identifying key campus contributors, searching frequently used words and/or hashtags, conducting survey research, and examining collected institutional data.

Planning: Goals and Strategy. It is essential to create a statement of desired goals and strategy to serve as a guide for drafting social media policies and/or guidelines. This step will focus the direction of the planning to include indicators of performance, accountability, and desired behaviors to address with social media governance at the institution.

Social Media Goals. It is important to align social media goals around current learning outcomes, campus objectives, and strategic plan. These goals should embody the core mission and values of the institution to build trust in the community. For consistency, this will require a social media advisory group to compile and review internal policies, codes of conduct, employee and student handbooks, IT protocols, and other organizational materials related to campus regulation. The regulations and current policies of the institution may already direct online behavior and use, which includes social media. Be informed, as to not duplicate a current policy. Some of this process may uncover the need to revise or augment current protocols set up within the institution, or identify gaps for guidelines and support.

Social Media Strategy. The actual strategy will be the specific recommendations and tactics to achieve the institutions' goals and outcomes identified after completing a social media assessment. By intentionally planning objectives and mapping out social media management, university leaders must set the university up for successful social media guideline and/or policy drafting. The social media policies and/or guidelines will communicate the campus's position and provide institutional stakeholders with a rationale for why these protocols were developed.

It is critical to outline key policy provisions to offer social media management across the institution. Strategic planning for social media use should take into account consistency, permissions and parameters, monitory issues endorsements, disclosures/disclaimers, copyrights and intellectual property rights of others, confidential/proprietary information, and spokesperson responsibility. To consider content creation and focus on the community participation, these governance documents need to add value to the institutional stakeholders and multiple audiences. A number of policy practices include full disclosure of roles behind the accounts, confidentiality protocols, and registering "official" institutional accounts for the campus social media directory. These suggestions offer ownership, endorse, and formally recognize how the university or college engages online.

Finally, a social media strategy should embody the goals and vision for effective campus communication and community development. The social media policies and/or guidelines should do more than just regulate dissemination of information across channels and platforms. In order to gain acceptance and trust among institutional stakeholders, potential concerns and challenges must be addressed during the drafting phases. Communicating and regularly updating institutional stakeholders on social media governance developments will ensure buy-in from the community of users during the implementation phase. Utilizing the campus community to solicit feedback, suggestions, and input for potential policies and/or guidelines is helpful. Transparency and open disclosure during the development phase will not only inform, but also remind campus stakeholders of social media governance significance.

Governance and Policy Drafting

Increasingly, institutional stakeholders are participating on these platforms to connect, form social connections, access information, communicate with one another, and more. As defined earlier in this chapter, the online community members collectively drive these platforms. Social media is more than just owning digital real estate, and it is not just another way to broadcast messages. That being said, the community on campus needs a form of governance that adheres to institutional policy, practices, and standards.

Social Media Policy.   A social media policy will be a standard document linked to institutional policies and governance protocols within the college or university. This serves as a legal record, and it is more than just an etiquette guide for institutional stakeholders to follow. Social media policies address prohibitions and regulatory compliances consistent with other conduct policies at postsecondary institutions. Common elements of a social media policy for all institutional stakeholders include

NEW DIRECTIONS FOR STUDENT SERVICES • DOI: 10.1002/ss

- A statement of institutional expectation for all to follow campus ethics guidelines
- A reminder that everyone will be held individually responsible for their posts and actions on the social Web, and if staff violate the law online, they and not the college or university are accountable;
- A disclaimer to remind institutional stakeholders should not officially represent or speak on the institution's behalf on social media; users should make it clear their thoughts are their own
- Transparency in interaction, stating their affiliation with the institution when required and providing authorship when appropriate on social media channels
- A statement reminding community users to respect all copyright and fair-use laws
- A reminder that academic and administrative staff are not to divulge information that is proprietary or confidential to the organization or its institutional stakeholders, including financial records, research, and student information related to local privacy laws
- A reminder of how all conduct reflects on the institution, so disrespectful conduct like ethnic slurs, insults, or hate speech will not be tolerated
- A privacy reminder that the Internet is forever and that whatever gets posted is usually searchable and findable by someone, so everyone should exercise discretion in their posts and interactions online.

Social media community managers at an institution should be involved in reviewing terms of service, privacy settings, legal policy, and platform features that could impact the institution's codes of conduct, students' rights and responsibilities, and/or organizational policies. Community managers and administrators responsible for institutional social media accounts need to focus on building relationships and creating conversations with campus stakeholders. It is recommended to have full-time staff (this might be a student, student, or faculty member) from an institution be responsible for divisional social media account(s). As a member of the campus community, this account and/or community manager should be expected to abide by current governance outlined by the college or university for expected behaviors, including but not limited to

- Students' rights and responsibilities
- Institutional code of conduct
- Communication, marketing, and privacy protocols
- Ethical research standards
- Athletic regulations
- Organization or leadership agreements for clubs, groups, and affiliations
- Privacy and freedom of information laws
- Human resource handbooks and
- IT, security, and computer policies.

New Directions for Student Services • DOI: 10.1002/ss

Copyright, attribution, and author identification should be outlined on institutional and personal social media account when possible. Unlike paid media, community user-generated content, that is, tweets, Facebook posts, YouTube videos, and more, are subject to copyright laws. Social media sites are not exempt from traditional copyright laws, copyright infringement, and intellectual property challenges, so it is critical to get the author's consent and attribution the work to comply with laws such as the federal Digital Millennium Copyright Act (DCMA). Provide disclaimers about user-generated content, with regards to privacy, profanity, racism, sexism or other derogatory. Identify content author(s) who are designated to provide resources, organize user-driven content, and draft materials for different social media and digital platforms. A guide for content authors will help maintain standards for what is appropriate content, similar to recommendations from the Harvard University governance model:

> Unless you specify otherwise, any and all works of authorship copyrightable by you and posted by you to any blog ("Content") are submitted under the terms of an Attribution–ShareAlike Creative Commons Public License. Under this license, you permit anyone to copy, distribute, display and perform your Content, royalty-free, on the condition that they credit your authorship each time they do so. You also permit others to distribute derivative works of your Content, but only if they do so under the same Attribution–ShareAlike license that governs your original Content (Harvard Blogs, 2014).

Modeling and mentoring appropriate and legal sharing practices in these environments provides examples for the community of users. It is important to be transparent with social media followers and readers, and offer attribution and authorship across social media channels.

These formal social media policies offer community users on campus transparency, disclosure, and confidence as to what they can and cannot say between their personal and institutional accounts. This legal document will help to set community standards, outline legal responsibilities, and regulate online behavior. Policies may also determine disciplinary actions for unsuitable conduct and online interactions. Often social media policies detail expectations for individual use versus institutional practices to outline examples for institutional stakeholders on these platforms.

Support for Implementation: Guiding Campus Community.   As social media governance documents are adopted, institutional users will seek administrative support to teach, offer programs, and frequent these social media platforms (Joosten, 2012). Offering open, transparent standards will vary by institution; however, outlining clear policies and/or guidelines provides instruction, permission, and direction for stakeholders who want to engage on these social spaces. It will be important to be transparent during social media governance drafting and implementation. Provide updates to social media governance-planning process, which might include solicitation for feedback, suggestions for practices, and comments to pending drafts. Be sure to connect institutional stakeholders to the goals identified after the assessment phase. By demonstrating how the social media governance model aligns with the campus strategic plan, staff may help to create a road map for process. Share the plan for development or revision of protocols, and seek input for the process along the way to make adoption easier and more effective.

The Nature and Infrastructure of Social Media Platforms Encourage Organic Interactions and Open Comments. The campus community should be afforded the opportunity to learn and develop on these social media mediums. Consider the challenges, needs, and gaps required to offer institutional support among different divisions on campus. This might be for teaching and learning, recruitment strategy, marketing campaigns, fundraising goals, or research scholarship. Scaffolding local outreach for social media use will not only encourage campus stakeholders to participate and get involved on social media channels, it can also model examples of effective program initiatives, helpful instructional strategies, distribution of research, and highlight active members connected to the institution.

Social Media Guidelines. To support social media policies, the institution may consider drafting a supporting etiquette and unwritten rules for the organization. Social media guidelines typically offer a number of "how to" guides and educational information to support effective social media usage and behavior. Social media guidelines offer colleges and universities a centralized location to train and educate members of the community. Academics are already using social media as a way to share information and resources, expand learning opportunities beyond the classroom environment, requesting assistance or feedback, offering suggestions, forming professional digital identities, and connecting and networking across multiple online social networks (Veletsianos, 2012). The campus community users will want to aggregate around common topics, shared events, and news related to the institution. It would be helpful to suggest methods for researching ideas, developing posts, writing content, providing useful examples, showcasing services, and offering additional educational support for social media management. Oftentimes social media guidelines offer suggestions for content ideas, posting tips, moderating comments, encouraging interactions, and sharing videos, images or photos on social media channels.

Social media guidelines will offer suggestions for posting on official institutional sites and channels, specifically with regards to tone, respect, and presence. To add quality content and value to the campus community, guidelines typically remind community managers to keep it interesting and entertaining as an active participant. Oftentimes there are suggestions for frequency of sharing content that current, accurate, and appropriate for the campus. It might even be helpful to share effective writing styles, lengths, logos, and identity when posting to particular platforms. Consider what other helpful tips, suggestions, and resources will help guide the behavior staff may want for the campus community.

Social Media Training and Support.   Effective institutional guidelines offer common areas to learn, train, teach, and develop social media organization of particular platforms. By creating social media guidelines reinforced with learning opportunities, staff may offer institutional stakeholders support, training, and mentoring for effective participation on these platforms. To implement social media at the institutional level successfully, campus leaders need to include the following items for the campus guidelines (adopted from Joosten, 2012, p. 84):

- Establish user groups and cohorts for campus community mentoring and modeling
- Offer technological and pedagogical instruction through campus workshops, recorded Web casts, and curated training resources
- Encourage pilots and programs that infuse social media into the design and development of each project
- Create a digital repository to showcase exemplars and suggested practices from the campus community
- Develop instructional guides that outline technical help and document evidence-based practices for social media teaching, service, and research scholarship
- Form a research hub to help provide evaluation and assessment for teaching, learning, and services using social media at the campus
- Offer centralized, institutional support that might include walk-ins, follow up, or further needs from a social media instructional training workshop or resource

Keep in mind, these social media guidelines and policies need to focus on presence and community building community, rather than promotion, marketing, and advocating for subscribers/followers. The campus is not interested in reading another bulletin board or being marketed to on social media channels. It is important to encourage participation; however, conversation, interests, and ideas will be essential for sustaining these communities. Specifics of the social media platforms and applications might change with technological updates; however governing documents should focus on behaviors and use by the campus population.

To organize information sharing and linking to other content at the institution, social media guidelines might provide strategies for linking information to other institutional accounts, aggregating social media channels, and encouraging cross posting to on social media platforms at a local institution. Encourage others to link to institutional Web sites and social media sites by including share buttons at the bottom of Web pages. Participation and engagement for a campus social media should be a consideration based on campus community interests and preferences. Central and "official" institutional accounts often organize a social media content calendar for sharing information, news, and interactions with institutional stakeholders to not overwhelm or monopolize the primary platforms for campus and to create interaction with the community members online.

Comments, posts, and threaded discussions indicate interaction and interest among the campus community. Some institutions offer specific directions for responding to and tracking comments on social media channels. All comments on social media channels can be forwarded, copied, and shared, and all responses from institutional accounts will represent the college or university. It is a good idea to have social media governance documents be inclusive of how to manage negative comments or feedback on social media platforms. Certain policies will outline protocols and disciplinary actions; however, social media guidelines should account for effective management of spam, flaming, trolling, and abusive/inappropriate behavior, such as hate language, personal attacks, and off-topic comments. Establish guidelines for disabling or removing community users, product advertising, or phishing on social media channels. For example, Cardinal Stritch University offers the following ways to moderate comments on their social media channels:

> Even the negative ones. A good philosophy for comments is to encourage thoughtful discussion; debate and differing viewpoints, with the understanding that all comments made must be civil, respectful, and appropriate for your audience. If comments are lewd, libelous, incite violence or are otherwise hurtful or hateful speech directed at either individuals or groups, Stritch employees who serve as account administrators reserve the right to delete such comments (Cardinal Stritch University, 2016).

It is also very important to be prepared to accept, moderate, and respond on a regular basis. This means community managers need to be part of the community first by listening and then responding in a timely fashion. Ensure community managers are reading and replying with clean and constructive interactions. This might involve asking follow-up questions if the comment is unclear, and ensuring account managers maintain a respectful tone in a response. Social etiquette can go a long way in these digital streams to be inclusive and support for the campus community.

For individual social media users, it will be important to address personal use of social media in policies and guidelines for institutional stakeholders. This could be a caution for mixing a personal social media account with a department/division account at the institution during business hours. Or it could include information on effective digital identify management and safety/privacy features for individual accounts. Often, community users are reminded not to associate their personal identity with that of the institution on personal sites, or at least to identify that their own opinion does not reflect that of the institution or that will bring the organization

Figure 6.1. Recommendations for social media guideline and policy development.

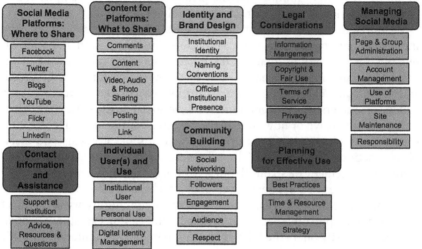

into disrepute. Social media guidelines should remind institutional stakeholders that harassment, cyberbullying, cyberstalking, and other unwanted online behaviors are not tolerated from any member of the campus community. It is also a good idea to remind institutional stakeholders to avoid the distribution of gossip, rumors, and unverified information.

For further examples and exemplars of social media policies and guidelines from postsecondary institutions, a social media advisory group can access and download the database of policy and guideline documents archived from research, and also review Appendix G: Recommendations for Social Media Guideline and Policy Development (Pasquini, 2014, pp. 124–155) for detailed inclusions for institutional policy considerations. The resulting nine categories and 36 topics (see Figure 6.1) will offer a social media advisory group a central reference point to direct their own policy development, revision, and writing.

Although the social media policy and/or guidelines are not all inclusive of the campus' needs, this is a solid starting point to direct focused research and planning for social media governance and support at the institution.

Conclusion

Social media policies and/or guidelines create a foundation for the community. Think about the way staff may craft policies, guidelines, and practices to build campus community online. Social media has the potential to influence campus participation, set standards for involvement, moderate interactions, and cultivate public engagement at institutions. It is critical for universities and colleges to consider social media governance and digital policies that reflect the values of the institution, in particular, acceptable campus stakeholder interactions, and effective strategies for knowledge sharing. Social media and digital technology guidance development will involve campus stakeholder participation to create appropriate protocols for use and to identify acceptable online behaviors. Digital and social media guidelines should enhance current institutional practices, and support the vision and development of campus community. As student affairs administrators and educators, this chapter provides the framework to begin, augment, or sustain efforts to engage the digital generation of students and professionals throughout the academy.

References

Blaschke, L. M. (2014). Using social media to engage and develop the online learner in self-determined learning. *Research in Learning Technology, 22*.

Cardinal Stritch University. (2016). Social media: Best practices. Retrieved from http://www.stritch.edu/Offices-and-Services/Marketing/Social-Media/Best-Practices/

Glendinning, I. (2014). Responses to student plagiarism in higher education across Europe. *International Journal for Educational Integrity, 10*(1), 4–20.

Hanna, R., Rohm, A., & Crittenden, V. L. (2011). We're all connected: The power of the social media ecosystem. *Business Horizons, 54*(3), 265–273.

Harvard Blogs. (2014, August 15). Terms of Use. Retrieved from http://blogs.harvard.edu/terms-of-use/

Holloway, M., & Boccelli, B. (2014, January 28). No snow day announcement met with Twitter backlash. *The Daily Illini*. Retrieved from http://www.dailyillini.com/news/campus/article_f63ad3cc-879e-11e3-a8db-001a4bcf6878.html

Joosten, T. (2012). *Social media for educators.* San Francisco, CA: Jossey Bass.

Joosten, T., Pasquini, L. A., & Harness, L. (2013). Guiding social media at our institutions. *Planning for Higher Education, 41*(2), 1–11.

Jouvenal, J., & Shapiro, T. R. (2015, May 6). Feminists at Mary Washington say they were threatened on Yik Yak. *The Washington Post*. Retrieved from http://www.washingtonpost.com/local/crime/feminists-at-mary-washington-say-they-were-threatened-on-yik-yak/2015/05/06/3d8d287a-f34a-11e4-b2f3-af5479e6bbdd_story.html

Junco, R. (2014). *Engaging students through social media: Evidence based practices for use in student affairs.* San Francisco, CA: Wiley/Jossey-Bass.

Kaplan, A. M., & Haenlein, M. (2010). Users of the world, unite! The challenges and opportunities of Social Media. *Business Horizons, 53*(1), 59–68.

Kingkade, T. (2015, May 14). Kennesaw State student told that waiting for an advisor is "harassing." *Huffington Post*. Retrieved from http://www.huffingtonpost.com/2015/05/14/kennesaw-state-advisor-its-bigger-than-ksu_n_7284748.html

McHale, R. (2012). *Navigating social media legal risks: Safeguarding your business.* Indianapolis, IN: Pearson Education.

Pasquini, L. A. (2014). Organizational identity and community values: Determining meaning in post-secondary education social media guideline and policy documents. Denton, Texas. UNT Digital Library. http://www.digital.library.unt.edu/ark:/67531/metadc700007/

Pasquini, L. A., & Evangelopoulos, N. (2015). Organizational identity, meaning, and values: Analysis of social media guideline and policy documents. In *the SMSociety '15*

Proceedings of the 2015 International Conference on Social Media & Society, Toronto, ON, Canada, 27–29 July. New York, NY: ACM. doi: 10.1145/2789187.2789198

Rodriguez, J. E. (2011). Social media use in higher education: Key areas to consider for educators. *Journal of Online Learning and Teaching, 7*(4). Retrieved from http://jolt.merlot.org/vol7no4/rodriguez_1211.htm

Salaita, S. R. (2015, October 5). Why I was fired. *The Chronicle of Higher Education.* Retrieved from http://chronicle.com/article/Why-I-Was-Fired/233640

Sandvig, C. (2015, May 8). What Facebook's "it's not our fault" study really means. *Wired.* Retrieved from http://www.wired.com/2015/05/facebook-not-fault-study/

Scott, P. R., & Jacka, J. M. (2011). *Auditing social media: A governance and risk guide.* Hoboken, NJ: John Wiley & Sons.

Selkie, E. (2015, March 23). Cyberbullying: A virtual menace takes its toll on college students. *The Conversation.* Retrieved from http://theconversation.com/cyberbullying-a-virtual-menace-takes-its-toll-on-college-students-38357

Smith, S. R. (2013). The connected learning environment. Retrieved from https://net.educause.edu/ir/library/pdf/PUB9013.pdf

Snoeijers, E. M., Poels, K., & Nicolay, C. (2014). #universitycrisis the impact of social media type, source, and Information on student responses toward a university crisis. *Social Science Computer Review.* doi: 0894439314525025.

Snyder, B. (2014, May 22). Universities want broader regulation of their communities' social media. *Fortune.* Retrieved from http://fortune.com/2014/05/22/universities-want-broader-regulation-of-their-communities-social-media/

Thomason, A. (2015, March 24). NASPA's annual conference was going well then Yik Yak showed up. *The Chronicle of Higher Education.* Retrieved from http://chronicle.com/blogs/ticker/naspas-annual-conference-was-going-well-then-yik-yak-showed-up/96089

Veletsianos, G. (2012). Higher education scholars' participation and practices on Twitter. *Journal of Computer Assisted Learning, 28*(4), 336–349.

Wang, Y., & Meiselwitz, G. (2015). *Social media and higher education: A literature review. Social Computing and Social Media, 9182,* 96–104.

Wile, R. (2015, November 14). The Yik Yak threat at Mizzou was the 40th issued at a U.S. school this year. *Fusion.* Retrieved from http://fusion.net/story/231081/mizzou-incident-shows-yik-yak-threats-have-now-become-a-standard-part-of-campus-life-in-america/

LAURA A. PASQUINI *is a lecturer with the Department of Learning Technologies in the College of Information at the University of North Texas and a research fellow with the Digital Learning and Social Media Research Group at Royal Roads University in Victoria, BC.*

NEW DIRECTIONS FOR STUDENT SERVICES • DOI: 10.1002/ss

INDEX

ORDER FORM SUBSCRIPTION AND SINGLE ISSUES

DISCOUNTED BACK ISSUES:

Use this form to receive 20% off all back issues of *New Directions for Student Services*.
All single issues priced at **$23.20** (normally $29.00)

TITLE	ISSUE NO.	ISBN
_____	_____	_____
_____	_____	_____
_____	_____	_____

*Call 1-800-835-6770 or see mailing instructions below. When calling, mention the promotional code JBNND
to receive your discount. For a complete list of issues, please visit www.josseybass.com/go/ndss*

SUBSCRIPTIONS: (1 YEAR, 4 ISSUES)

☐ New Order   ☐ Renewal

U.S.	☐ Individual: $89	☐ Institutional: $335
CANADA/MEXICO	☐ Individual: $89	☐ Institutional: $375
ALL OTHERS	☐ Individual: $113	☐ Institutional: $409

*Call 1-800-835-6770 or see mailing and pricing instructions below.
Online subscriptions are available at www.onlinelibrary.wiley.com*

ORDER TOTALS:

Issue / Subscription Amount: $ _____

Shipping Amount: $ _____
(for single issues only – subscription prices include shipping)

Total Amount: $ _____

SHIPPING CHARGES:

First Item $6.00
Each Add'l Item $2.00

*(No sales tax for U.S. subscriptions. Canadian residents, add GST for subscription orders. Individual rate subscriptions must
be paid by personal check or credit card. Individual rate subscriptions may not be resold as library copies.)*

BILLING & SHIPPING INFORMATION:

☐ **PAYMENT ENCLOSED:** *(U.S. check or money order only. All payments must be in U.S. dollars.)*

☐ **CREDIT CARD:** ☐ VISA ☐ MC ☐ AMEX

Card number _____Exp. Date_____

Card Holder Name_____Card Issue # _____

Signature _____Day Phone_____

☐ **BILL ME:** *(U.S. institutional orders only. Purchase order required.)*

Purchase order # _____
Federal Tax ID 13559302 • GST 89102-8052

Name_____

Address_____

Phone_____ E-mail_____

Copy or detach page and send to: **John Wiley & Sons, One Montgomery Street, Suite 1000,
San Francisco, CA 94104-4594**

Order Form can also be faxed to: **888-481-2665**

PROMO JBNND

The Jossey-Bass Student Leadership Competencies Database

How do you know you're teaching the leadership skills your students will need?

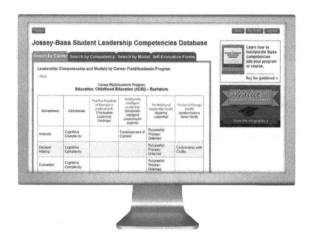

Bridge the gap between leadership development and career preparation by teaching your students the skills required by their academic programs and future career fields. Use this free online tool, covering the four major models of student leadership development, to align your course or program to accreditation requirements.

Try it now at **www.josseybass.com/go/studentleadershipcompetencies**

A Wiley Brand